THE SPIRITED VEGETARIAN

Over 100 Recipes Made Lively with Wine and Spirits

PAULETTE MITCHELL

RODALE

Printed in the United States of America
Rodale Inc. makes every effort to use acid-free ∞, recycled paper ♻.

Illustrations by Dennis Clouse/Cyclone Design
Book design by Judith Abbate/Abbate Design

Library of Congress Cataloging-in-Publication Data

Mitchell, Paulette.
    The spirited vegetarian : over 100 recipes made lively with wine and spirits / Paulette Mitchell.
        p.   cm.
    Includes index.
    ISBN-13 978–1–57954–970–1 paperback
    ISBN-10 1–57954–970–5 paperback
    1. Vegetarian cookery.   2. Cookery (Wine)   3. Cookery (Liquors)   I. Title.
    TX837.M653   2005
    641.5'636—dc22   2004026492

Distributed to the trade by Holtzbrinck Publishers

2   4   6   8   10   9   7   5   3   1   paperback

We inspire and enable people to improve their lives and the world around them
For more of our products visit **rodalestore.com** or call 800-848-4735

To Brett, my 21-year-old son.
From high chair to computer chair,
From tabletop to laptop.
I was the teacher.
Now I am the student.

Contents

 # Preface

It was a chilly fall night when I gathered together ingredients from the farmers' market. The windows steamed over with a cozy glaze as I caramelized onions, chopped tomatoes and sweet bell peppers, and peeled a lovely acorn squash. I stirred vegetable stock into the pot and added some dried fruit and black beans. The simmering stew celebrated a palette of brilliant colors and earthy flavors, a perfect autumn welcome for my guests arriving any minute. But, as I tasted my creation, I knew it needed something. Not salt or pepper. No more sage (that was distinct enough). Plenty of garlic already. On a whim, I stirred in some dry sherry. Just a dash of spirit gave that dish its soul—and the concept of *The Spirited Vegetarian* was born.

Food and wine can be delicious on their own, but they're even more interesting when they intermingle in the mouth as an extraordinary flavor pairing. The same thing can happen in the pot, when food and wine marry to conceive a remarkable dish. The French, of course, seem to know instinctively when and how much "spirit" to add to a recipe. Think of Coq au Vin and Beef Bourguignonne. Consider, too, the classic wine-enhanced sauces of Italy.

Chefs often boost the taste of meat-based dishes with wine and spirits. Vegetarian cooks, too, can augment recipes, either boldly or subtly, with a variety of spirits. Over the last 30 years or so, vegetarian cooking has evolved into a cuisine that stands proudly on its own, defined not so much by the absence of meat but by its creative approach to ingredients and flavors. The vegetable and legume kingdom is vast, and the possibilities for vegetarians (or anyone who appreciates a meatless meal now and then) are open to a world of interpretation. Talented cooks who avoid meat are becoming wildly innovative, incorporating the flavor systems and influences of the world's cuisines. It makes sense that as cooks explore various approaches, they should consider integrating all of the elements available to them—and that brings us to wine and spirits.

Whether you eat vegetarian every day or once a week, a touch of wine can transform the humblest of dishes into the most luxurious, and food prepared with spirits always seems to have an air of celebration. Becoming a *spirited vegetarian* is a simple way to add sophistication to vegetarian fare and to make comfort food elegant. Alcohol improves flavors in such a way that you can make many delectable sauces without adding cream. Best of all, spirits open up a whole new category of taste sensations, which can make your cooking more creative.

The recipes in *The Spirited Vegetarian*—the first and only vegetarian cookbook integrating wine and spirits as essential ingredients—are culled from classic and contemporary creations, many influenced by my own travels through Europe, Asia, the South Pacific, and the United States. Backed by inspiration from my local farmers' market and a favorite wine shop, the range of recipes is indeed lively. If you are a novice, the simple preparations will appeal to you, while experienced gourmets will appreciate the complex flavors of specialty ingredients.

Wine and spirits can greatly enhance many types of dishes because there are so many styles to choose from: soft or acidic, fruity or spicy, high or low in alcohol, sparkling or still, fortified or not, dry or sweet. Sometimes, the liquor is a key flavor element. Other times, it is a subtle component of the dish. Wine and spirits can improve both savory and sweet dishes. They add appealing undertones to hearty dishes in the winter as well as to the refreshing meals we crave when the temperature soars.

Nearly all of these creations will also delight nonvegetarians when used as accompaniments to meat. For strict vegetarians, many of these recipes not only are meatless but also are made without animal-derived foods, including dairy products (butter, cheese, milk) and eggs. I've identified these recipes, including those that can easily be adapted to become vegan.

Spirited vegetarian dishes include the whole repertoire, from appetizers, soups, salads, and main courses to desserts and snacks. Classic cheese fondue made creamy with Sauvignon Blanc (*page 35*) is personalized with homemade Basil Pesto (*page 36*). Sweet Strawberry-Madeira Soup (*page 81*) makes a welcome addition to a sizzling summer brunch, while Fennel and Vegetable Soup with Sherried Mushrooms (*page 64*) is sure to please guests on a frosty night. A bread salad is intriguing with Sangiovese Vinaigrette (*page 93*), and a green salad has panache when assembled with Pears Poached in Crème de Cassis (*page 87*) and walnut vinaigrette. Globe-spanning entrées range from a hearty Gingered Squash Risotto with Glazed Pecans and Fried Sage (*page 113*) to a Cabernet Sauvignon–infused Vegetarian Cassoulet (*page 162*). Humble beans become an elegant stew flavored with an earthy red wine in Cannellini Bean Bourguignonne (*page 128*). No one will miss the meat in Tuscan Porcini Ragù with Spinach Fettuccine (*page 138*) prepared with just the right amount of woodsy mushrooms and Sangiovese. And there's a spirited dessert for everyone's taste, from Chocolate-Cherry Bread Pudding with Sherry Cream (*page 176*) to quickly prepared Limoncello Ice Cream (*page 190*). The choices are sophisticated, stylish, elegant, and intriguing, yet simple and quick to prepare.

I've been creating recipes for 2 decades while teaching cooking classes and writing 11 cookbooks, but I must acknowledge that developing these recipes has actually changed the way I cook. It's become natural for me to incorporate wine and spirits in my vegetarian dishes, and I love the results. I hope you, too, will come to appreciate the benefits of including wine and spirits in your repertoire. In addition to more than 100 recipes, you'll find tips on ingredients and techniques, as well as the kitchen wisdom that my readers appreciate and have come to expect.

Acknowledgments

SINCERE THANKS to my agent Jane Dystel, my editors Margot Schupf and Shea Zukowski, as well as the entire team at Rodale, each of whom contributed their talents to this project.

And to many others who tasted, tested, shared favorite recipes, imparted wisdom, and inspired me: Brett Mitchell, Darryl Trones, Judy Witts Francini, Lisa Genis, Michael Hochhalter, Kristine Igo, Raghavan Iyer, Fran LeBahn, Barb Kennedy, Leslie Levich Knight, Emilie Richardson, Jane Smith Schellhas, Peggy Struble, Lis Viehweg, Claudia Wagner, Carla Waldemar, and Marie Wintergerst.

 # Introduction

In my opinion, cooking is an artistic endeavor that does not lend itself to strict rules. Yet, as I created the *spirited vegetarian* recipes for this book, I was delighted to discover a few unexpected pleasures. For example, usually wine and spirits contribute their unique characteristics to a dish, but in some recipes I found that the spirit simply enlivens foods and allows them to more fully release their own flavors.

I hope that you are able to discover similar delight as you cook from this book. After all, there's really nothing intimidating about selecting wine or cooking with it. It's not important that you *fully* understand the principles for matching food to wine in order to use these recipes, or in order to adapt them to use wine you may have on hand.

In my initial recipe testing, I worked with a limited number of basic wines, such as Sangiovese as my dry red and Pinot Grigio as my white, because they have high levels of acidity, an important element in many recipes. Later, with the help of Kristine Igo, my wine advisor at a favorite wine shop, I determined the optimum type of wine for each recipe, taking into account the wines' distinct personalities.

As I retested and fine-tuned the recipes, I recognized the importance of adding the rich flavors offered by wines such as Cabernet Sauvignon and Chardonnay. Other dishes benefited from the distinct fruitiness of Gewürztraminer or the plumminess of Merlot. And I found that citrusy white wines, such as Riesling, add much the same character as a squeeze of lemon.

What's most important, in my opinion, is that you follow your instincts. Use your "flavor memory" of the primary ingredients and the qualities they will contribute to the dish as you take a sip of wine to judge the compatibility.

To help along the way as you decide which wines to serve with the main course recipes, I've offered pairing suggestions to make your *spirited vegetarian* meals complete. You'll notice that it is not necessary to serve the same wine to accompany the dish that you use to prepare it. If you'd like, serve a premium bottle for drinking and cook with a less expensive wine that has similar characteristics. The *Spirited Vegetarian* Wine Chart on page 12 can be used to select alternatives for drinking as well as for cooking.

Stocking Up and Storing Wisely

With so many wines available, the decision of what to purchase may seem challenging. So, let's start by covering what *not* to purchase, and for that I offer this unbending rule: "Cooking never improves a bad wine." I do not recommend using any wines labeled "cooking wine" because they contain additives and are overly salty. Likewise, wine vinegar is the perfect ingredient in many salad dressings, but it cannot substitute for wine in the recipes in this book since it is made by adding bacteria to sherry, which turns it into an acid with a sour flavor.

My guideline is simple: If you can't drink it, don't cook with it. However, cooking doesn't require that you invest in a fine vintage. There are many excellent, reasonably priced wines perfect for cooking.

Since we all know that spontaneous meals require advance planning, I advise keeping on hand four bottles that should see you through most recipes: a dry and a semisweet red, as well as a dry and a semisweet white. Wine always keeps best in an unopened bottle, which should be stored on its side in a dark, cool place (about 65°F is ideal). Extreme temperature fluctuations will destroy a wine's character.

At the opposite end of "advance planning" is the age-old cooks' rule to use up what you have. And though it's always preferable to cook with a just-opened bottle, many see cooking with wine as an opportunity to use up wine opened the night before or several days earlier. But choose the recipe carefully. The wines called for in my recipes were selected for their specific characteristics, which are most prominent when a wine is just opened. As soon as wine is exposed to oxygen, its flavor begins to change. Over time, it will lose its acidity, tannin, and fruitiness.

If you wish to cook with a wine that's been previously opened, taste it first. If you detect any hint of "off," musty, or vinegary flavors, it's best to discard the wine. These undesirable characteristics would become more concentrated with cooking.

With this discussion of using wines at the peak of flavor, you may be wondering how I was able to keep opened wines in the best possible condition as I developed the recipes for this book. I found that a vacuum wine saver, which is designed to remove excess air from the partially full bottle, helps to maintain the flavor for up to 2 weeks. Another gadget allows you to "gas" wine by introducing a weighty combination of nitrogen and carbon dioxide that pushes the lighter oxygen out of the bottle. To minimize air space, some cooks swear by pouring leftover wine to the top of a smaller, scrupulously clean container with a tight-fitting lid, such as an empty plastic water bottle. Whichever method you choose, it's important to seal the bottle tightly, refrigerate the wine, and use it as soon as possible. An exception is fortified wines, such as port and sherry. Because they are partially oxidized to begin with, they have a longer life once opened and can be stored either in or out of the refrigerator.

Cooking with Wine

Traditionally, there have been strict guidelines about matching food and wine, many of which are often applied to cooking with wine. The old rule about white wine with light foods and red wine with dark foods makes sense when you consider the appearance of a finished dish. But in terms of flavor, this theory emerged when white wines were consistently light and fruity and red wines were usually tannic and full-bodied. Today, winemaking has evolved to the point that these distinctions are far less clear. While it's still true that the apple, pear, and citrus flavors found in many white wines rarely show up in reds, and the currant, cherry, and tobacco flavors of red grapes usually do not appear in whites, both wines share many flavor characteristics and can be spicy, buttery, leathery, earthy, or floral.

As we have developed a better understanding of wines' properties and have gained access to a wide variety of wines from around the world, many people have also begun to depart from the traditional idea that wines from a particular region go best with dishes from the same area. Clearly, the tendency in recent years has been to experiment more and relax restrictions. With this open approach to pairing in mind as you prepare *spirited vegetarian* recipes, I suggest that you consider the following basic principles:

A little flavor can go a long way. The elements that you taste when you sip wine will be reflected in the dish. Just a few tablespoons of wine will make a difference in some dishes; large amounts may not be necessary. Fortified wines, such as Madeira, port, and sherry, have distinctive, strong flavors, so it's important to add them prudently. To a degree, wine, like salt and pepper, can be added "to taste." Add extra gradually, however, because using much more than is called for in a recipe may upset the balance of a dish.

Balance is important. Take into account the intensity of flavors, matching the assertiveness of the wine to the dominant flavor of the ingredients in the dish. Robust spirits overwhelm mild and delicate foods, while strong-flavored foods benefit from the addition of a hearty, full-bodied wine. For the characteristics of the wine to be noticeable, the sweetness or tartness of the finished dish should be less intense than that of the wine.

Flavor is a two-way street. In food and wine pairing, as well as in cooking, the complexities of a given dish will also affect the flavor of the wine. For example, sweetness makes wine taste stronger and more acidic, while acid in food makes wine become milder and sweeter. Salt subdues bitter and acidic flavors and allows others to come forward. Peppers, chiles, and hot spices accentuate the flavor of alcohol and are challenging ingredients for incorporating wine; highly seasoned dishes are best with wines that are fruity and lower in alcohol.

Adjust for acidity. Acidic wines such as Sangiovese pair well with acidic foods, such as tomatoes. However, acidity can become potent, so avoid cooking acidic foods with tart, very dry white wines. Along the same lines, fat mellows acidity, so full-bodied wines, which may overwhelm delicate flavors, are best in robust, rich, higher-fat dishes, such as cream sauces.

Use dry wine for savory dishes and sweet wine for desserts. In a dry wine or sherry, the sugar has been converted to alcohol during fermentation, and this will be evident in the completed dish. Sweet, or "cream," sherry and sweet wines, such as Sauternes and sweet Marsala, have residual sugar and taste best with sweet foods such as fruit. Keep in mind that sugar is intensified in cooking, so be sure to add sweet wines with a gentle hand.

Consider color. Because red wines add color as well as flavor to a dish, they often are combined with dark-colored foods, including tomatoes and some beans, such as kidney beans and fava beans. White wines are often used for light-colored dishes. In fact, you'll find that the color of white vegetables may be preserved and brightened by the acidity of white wine. Garlic and onions are naturally wine-friendly and will go with either reds or whites; the same is true for mushrooms.

Consider how wine will affect the cooking process. Wines nearly always should be cooked and will affect *how* a dish cooks. For example, when cheese is combined with wine, as in Cheese Fondue with Basil Pesto (*page 35*), the alcohol lowers the boiling point and helps to prevent the cheese from curdling when heated. To avoid curdling in other recipes, it may be necessary to add the wine before the cream and simmer to reduce the acidity. Remove the pan from the heat when adding the cream, and reheat with caution, taking care not to let the mixture come to a boil. The exceptions to the cooking rule are Champagne and sparkling wines, which can be added to a chilled dish just before serving to showcase their effervescence, and liqueurs can successfully be added to recipes without cooking.

Taste and adjust flavors. In general, the astringent, tannic properties of some red wines are the most challenging to use in recipes. If a dish seems to taste too harsh or acidic after adding the wine and cooking, add a little white or brown sugar to mellow the flavors.

Avoid changing the liquid ratios. To adapt a recipe that is already in your repertoire, you can substitute wine for part of the liquid ingredients. Keep in mind that very spicy or sour dishes are among the few that wine doesn't improve.

If you must avoid cooking with alcohol, substitute wisely. One question that I'm consistently asked when teaching culinary classes regards residual alcohol—the amount that remains after cooking. Numerous studies offer estimates, yet there is no precise answer because there are so many variables. In wine- or spirit-flavored dishes that are not heated, such as some desserts, there is some alcohol loss through evaporation, especially if the food is left uncovered. Food scientists also conclude that long, slow simmering eliminates more alcohol than adding the wine or liqueur toward the end of the cooking process. Yet a very small amount of alcohol always remains, and this is an important factor for those wishing to avoid all alcohol. I have not found a non-alcoholic wine that I would use for cooking. A better substitution is to replace the measure with another liquid, such as vegetable stock, fruit juice, or water, taking care to select a liquid compatible with the other ingredients in the recipe.

TECHNIQUES FOR *THE SPIRITED VEGETARIAN*

As I've mentioned, the intensity and taste of a wine may be altered by the cooking procedure. For example, when wine is added to the pan and then just briefly warmed, the alcohol flavor remains. Longer cooking, on the other hand, evaporates much of the alcohol and intensifies other characteristics of the wine. Therefore, the same wine can offer different flavors. Because wine presents such versatility, adding wine in several stages of the cooking process leads to greater flavor complexity.

To help you anticipate how these changes occur, here is a quick explanation of the wine-related cooking techniques used in these recipes:

Deglaze—This technique results in the base for many fine sauces and is done by adding liquid, such as wine, to the pan after sautéing ingredients. A wooden spoon is used to stir and scrape the bottom of the pan in order to dissolve the congealed and flavorful juices that have formed during cooking. As the liquid heats, the glaze that emerges is typically reduced to further concentrate the flavors. For more about reduction, see page 8.

Glaze—This procedure is used to create a flavorful and shiny glaze on foods. Wine is combined with other ingredients, such as butter, and brushed onto a dish as it cooks on the stove top, roasts, or bakes. As the liquid evaporates, a thin, glossy coating forms on the foods in the pan.

Macerate—This technique requires soaking fruit in wine, liqueur, or other spirits with sugar or sugar syrup. The process develops flavors and draws out the juices of uncooked fruits, so it's best to use soft, naturally juicy fruits such as berries. Use a spirit you enjoy because the fruit also absorbs the macerating liquid's flavor.

Keep in mind that macerating with red wine alters the color of fruit. Also, if red wine is used, a generous addition of sugar may be required, unless the wine is already sweet. Port, for example, requires no addition of sugar. Because of chemical reactions caused by the acid in wine, it's best to use glass or ceramic containers for macerating.

Poach—Poaching is done by cooking food in a liquid heated to just below the simmering point. The perfect temperature, around 180°F, creates a quivering of the liquid's surface and a slightly moving bubble at the edge of the pan. Sometimes the poaching liquid is reduced after fruit, for example, has been removed, to make a thick, rich-flavored sauce.

Reduce—In reduction, the wine, and often other liquid ingredients, are brought to a boil; then they're immediately turned down to a simmer, left uncovered, and stirred occasionally. They're slowly cooked down, or "reduced," to the point where the wine's flavor and aroma become concentrated.

Bringing wine to a simmer evaporates much of the alcohol. Reducing the wine also accentuates a wine's acidity, tannin, and oak flavors. But be aware that any flaws in the wine will become concentrated as well. And if reduced for too long, the acid in a wine will turn to bitterness and the sugar will start to caramelize. Therefore, when reducing high-tannin wines, it's especially important to remember to avoid cooking at a full boil because it will overconcentrate tannins.

Sweet wines lose their floral perfume if over-reduced, and fortified wines are concentrates to begin with, so they are rarely reduced further. Both sweet and fortified wines are generally added toward the end of the cooking period.

Three other tips for success: Watch the pan closely as your sauce is reducing; once a reduction sauce is finished, don't try to hold it over low heat (it will continue to reduce); and do not add unreduced wine to a finished sauce.

Simmer—This technique involves cooking the wine with other ingredients to mellow and blend the flavors. The heat should be low enough so that tiny bubbles just begin to break the surface. The pan is generally covered so that the liquid does not evaporate.

WINE TERMINOLOGY

If cooking with wine is new for you, I suggest finding a good wine merchant who can assist you in selecting the appropriate wine for your *spirited vegetarian* recipes. Here are a few terms used in my ingredient lists and in the chart on page 12, which also will come in handy when making wine selections.

Acidity—Tartness derived from fruit acids, which occurs naturally in wine. Acidity can be more pronounced in some wines as a result of growing conditions or winemaking processes.

Aroma—The predominant smell of a wine, including the fragrance of the grape itself, of the fermentation process, and sometimes of the oak barrels in which the wine was made or aged. Fruit aromas are generally more pronounced in younger wines.

Balance—The ratio of a wine's components, including fruitiness, sweetness, acidity, tannin, and alcohol content. A balanced wine has harmony, with no single element predominating.

Body—The weight or fullness of a wine on the palate, which is influenced by acidity, tannin, and the level of alcohol. Wines are described as ranging from light-bodied to full-bodied. For both drinking and cooking, a wine's "weight" should be in line with the "weight" of the dish. For example, use a rich, full-bodied white wine such as Chardonnay in a cream sauce and a light-bodied wine such as Pinot Grigio in a brothy wild mushroom soup.

Dry—Used to describe a wine with no sweetness in its profile. In a fully dry wine, all the sugar has been converted to alcohol during fermentation. A medium-dry or semisweet wine has some residual sugar.

Earthy—The taste or aroma of soil in wine, which can be a component of a wine's complexity.

Fortified—A wine is fortified when the winemaker adds brandy or a neutral spirit in order to boost alcohol content and stop fermentation (often before the sugar has been converted, leaving the wine sweet). Natural fermentation results in between 7 and 10 percent alcohol; fortified wines generally are between 17 and 21 percent alcohol. Some of the most common fortified wines are Madeira, dry sherry, sweet vermouth, Ruby Port, and Marsala, and they are used in these recipes.

Fruity—Aromas and flavors that come from the grape rather than from the winemaking process. Apple, apricot, blackberry, cherry, citrus, and plum are several of the most common fruit flavors used to describe a wine. Don't confuse "fruity" with "sweet." Ripe, jammy aromas are fruity components of some dry wines.

Herbal—Describes the aromas and flavors of some wines. Herbal aromas or flavors include lavender, mint, rosemary, thyme, savory, and earthy.

Jammy and plummy—Slightly cooked flavors of jam rather than of fresh fruit. Jamminess or plumminess is often a characteristic of red wines from hot climates.

Oaky—The smell or taste of the oak cask in which the wine was made or aged. Oak notes can include vanilla, clove, cinnamon, cedar, smoke, toast, bourbon, and coffee.

Soft—Low in tannin and/or acidity. Having a waterlike texture in the mouth.

Sweet—Wines with significant residual sugar.

Tannins—These are the astringent substances found in the seeds, skins, and stems of grapes. Tannins can also come from the oak barrels in which certain wines are aged, which is why even some white wines, which are made without grape skins, have tannins. These elements leave a slightly bitter aftertaste, similar to that found in tea leaves. You can detect tannins by the dry sensation in your mouth and the back of your throat. Wines with noticeable tannins are referred to as *tannic.*

Varietal—Many wines are labeled by the varietal, which is the actual grape that grows on the vine, such as Cabernet and Chardonnay. Federal law stipulates that a wine may take a varietal name if 75 percent or more of the grapes used were of that variety. Some wines are 100 percent one type of grape, but many are improved by blending.

Selecting the Wine

The chart on pages 12 and 13, which includes the wines called for in my recipes, describes the effects various wines have on food. It will be helpful if you choose to make substitutions. The lists are divided into reds and whites, which are arranged in a hierarchy from light- to full-bodied.

In the New World, including America, Australia, South Africa, and New Zealand, wines are labeled by their varietal names. In Europe, the finest wines are known by their geographic or Old World appellation. For example, white and red wine from the Burgundy region of France may both be labeled as Burgundies, while Chardonnay and Pinot Noir are the major grapes grown there. In the following lists and in my recipes, I've included all the information—whether variety or appellation—you'll need to choose the right wine. Keep in mind that many wines are actually blends of several grapes; the primary grape offers the predominant flavor.

The *Spirited Vegetarian* Wine Chart

Red Wines

Light to medium body

Soft tannins. Fruit flavor. Add subtle fruit qualities. Also good for poaching.

BEAUJOLAIS (FRANCE), **GAMAY NOIR, VALPOLICELLA** (ITALY)

Affordable substitutions: **BARDOLINO** (ITALY), **NOUVEAU BEAUJOLAIS**

Pronounced acidity. The ultimate red for cooking. Use to complement tomatoes and tomato sauces.

SANGIOVESE, CHIANTI (OR OTHER TUSCAN RED WINE), **BARBERA**

Affordable substitution: **SANGIOVESE** DESIGNATED WINE FROM ITALY

Medium body

Light to medium tannins. Fruity and aromatic. Add a sharper counternote to rich, savory dishes.

PINOT NOIR, BURGUNDY ROUGE (FRENCH PINOT NOIR)

Affordable substitutions: **CÔTES DU RHÔNE** (FRANCE)

Full body

High alcohol. Medium tannins. Ripe-jammy fruit flavor. Equivalent to a fruit compote ingredient. Add a sweet aroma and can serve as a less-sweet alternative to port.

SHIRAZ (AUSTRALIA), **RED ZINFANDEL** (CALIFORNIA), **MERLOT**

Affordable substitutions: **CABERNET/MERLOT BLEND** FROM WASHINGTON STATE

High alcohol. Pronounced tannins. Savory and spicy flavor. Add a peppery character and increase the "weight" of the food.

CABERNET SAUVIGNON, BORDEAUX ROUGE (FRANCE), **SYRAH, TEMPRANILLO** (SPAIN), **NEBBIOLO** (ITALY)

Affordable substitutions: **CHILEAN CABERNET SAUVIGNON, ARGENTINE MALBEC**

Fortified Wines

Full body

High alcohol. High in sugar. Add maximum weight and flavor to a dish.

MADEIRA, PORT (SPAIN), **SHERRY** (PORTUGAL)

Affordable substitutions: **PORTS** FROM AUSTRALIA OR CALIFORNIA

WHITE WINES

LIGHT TO MEDIUM BODY

Dry with subtle acids and mild flavors. Add just a dash of acidity and alcohol.

PINOT GRIGIO/PINOT GRIS
Affordable substitutions: **BORDEAUX BLANC** (FRANCE)

Dry with pronounced acidity and mineral characteristics. Offer the acidity of citrus as well as a fruit and mineral character. Good to counter the weightiness of cheese sauces.

SAUVIGNON BLANC (THE MOST ACID IS FOUND IN NEW ZEALAND'S **SAUVIGNON BLANC** OR **FRENCH SANCERRE**), **DRY RIESLING** (ALSATIAN), **GRÜNER VELTLINER** (AUSTRIA)
Affordable substitution: **SAUVIGNON BLANC** (CHILE)

MEDIUM BODY

Semisweet. Aromatic and lushly fruity. The ultimate white for cooking. Acidity livens flavors like a dash of citrus.

RIESLING (GERMANY, AUSTRALIA, OR CALIFORNIA), **GEWÜRZTRAMINER, VOUVRAY** (FRENCH CHENIN BLANC)
Affordable substitutions: **JOHANNISBERG RIESLING** (FROM WASHINGTON STATE), **CHARDONNAY** (AUSTRALIA)

FULL BODY

Dry. High alcohol. Richly flavored with oak-aged tannins. Oak aging offers a warm, caramelized character. A nice complement to cream or cheese in recipes.

CHARDONNAY (CALIFORNIA), **WHITE BURGUNDY** (FRANCE), MOST BARREL-AGED WINES
Affordable substitutions: **CÔTES DU RHÔNE BLANC** (FRANCE), **CHARDONNAY** (CHILE OR ARGENTINA)

SPARKLING WINES

MEDIUM BODY

Bubbly. May be sweet or dry. Add a dash of frizzante.

DRY: **CHAMPAGNE,** DOMESTIC SPARKLING WINES (BRUT STYLE) SWEET: **PROSECCO** OR **MOSCATO** (ITALY)
Affordable substitutions: DRY: **CAVA** (SPAIN) SWEET: **ASTI SPUMANTE** (CALIFORNIA)

DESSERT-STYLE WINES

FULL BODY

Very sweet. Offer sugar and honey character. Use for caramelizing, deglazing, or poaching fruit.

MUSCAT, SAUTERNES (FRANCE), **EISWEIN** (GERMANY)
Affordable substitutions: **MUSCAT** OR **ICE WINE** FROM CALIFORNIA, CANADA, OR AUSTRALIA

COOKING WITH OTHER SPIRITS

Like wines, liqueurs can be used to contribute sweetness, color, and flavor to a recipe. You can even make your own liqueur, such as **Limoncello** (*page 188*) or **Coffee-Flavored Liqueur** (*page 191*).

When cooking with intensely flavored liqueurs, it's important not to add too much, as they can easily overpower the other flavors in a dish. At the same time, because of their high alcohol content, their flavors can dissipate quickly when exposed to heat and air, so it is sometimes desirable to remove the pan from the heat before stirring in a liqueur.

When using other liquors, such as rum or vodka, allow enough cooking time to remove the alcohol's harsh taste. This can take up to 30 minutes in a recipe that is simmering or baking. As you might expect, full-bodied liquors contribute more flavor than their lighter versions. For example, dark rum offers more flavor than golden, or light, rum.

THE *SPIRITED VEGETARIAN'S* LIQUOR CABINET

In addition to wine, here are some suggestions for spirits you may wish to have on hand to make the recipes in this book. Many are available in small bottles or even single-serving miniature bottles, which may be enough for some of the recipes. Opened bottles, which are tightly closed, can be stored at room temperature indefinitely.

Flavored Liqueurs

Liqueurs are sweetened spirits (whiskey, vodka, brandy, or rum) infused with fruit, herbs, nuts, or spices. Buy a trusted brand so you are sure of getting the real thing and not a liqueur made with chemical flavorings. Here's a rundown of the liqueurs used in my recipes:

- *Orange-flavored liqueurs* ~ Grand Marnier (made from Cognac), Cointreau (less sweet than Grand Marnier), Triple Sec
- *Black currant–flavored liqueur* ~ Crème de cassis
- *Hazelnut-flavored liqueur* ~ Frangelico
- *Almond-flavored liqueur* ~ Amaretto di Saronno
- *Chocolate-flavored liqueurs* ~ Crème de cacao, Godiva
- *Coffee-flavored liqueur* ~ Kahlúa

Brandies

Brandy is a generic term for a spirit that is distilled from the juice, fruit, and pulp of any kind of fruit. The most common form of brandy is made from grapes that are distilled, aged in oak barrels, and transferred to glass jars after maturation. Here's a brief overview of the types available:

- *Cognac* ~ The most famous and elegant brandy, from the Charente-Maritime area in France; maturation takes place in oak casks for a minimum of 30 months
- *B & B* ~ Proprietary name for a blend of Bénédictine and brandy that is less sweet than many liqueurs
- *Fruit brandies* ~ There are a number of brandies that are made from fermented fruits other than grapes, including apple (Calvados), apricot, and cherry (referred to as Kirsch or Kirschwasser in Switzerland and Germany)

Other Spirits

A number of other spirits lend themselves well to the dishes in this book. Here is a brief description of each that appears in my recipes.

Tequila—A colorless liquor made by fermenting and distilling the sweet sap of the agave plant. Tequila is named after its city of origin in Mexico.

Vodka—A liquor made in varying strengths. One-hundred-proof vodka is a neutral spirit used for making liqueurs. Flavored vodkas, such as lemon vodka, are also available.

Rum—Produced from molasses, rum is the by-product of manufacturing raw sugar from sugar cane. Light rum is matured in pale ash-wood barrels for just 1 year and is then transferred to stainless steel tanks to age longer. The fuller-bodied dark (or black) types are in the barrel for 3 years to as long as 20 years. Either can be used in most recipes.

KITCHEN EQUIPMENT

It's not necessary to have special equipment for preparing the recipes in this book. It is important to note, however, that the acid in wine reacts with certain metals, such as aluminum and cast iron, creating a metallic taste. If pans of these materials are lined, they are fine for cooking with wine. The same is true for anodized aluminum, which does not react with acid. Nonstick pans, also, are safe.

The pan I use for my soups is a good-quality, stainless steel Dutch oven, which I prefer to a stockpot. The Dutch oven provides a large, flat surface that allows vegetables to cook in a single layer, and the wide pan opening makes it easy to add ingredients and check them as they cook. You'll need a tight-fitting lid so the liquid won't evaporate as the soup simmers. The Dutch oven can double as a pot for cooking pasta.

My other most frequently used pan is my large (12", 5-quart) sauté pan. The straight sides, as opposed to the slanted sides of a skillet, make the pan ideal for recipes calling for added liquid. You'll also find uses for large and medium skillets and saucepans, all with lids, which are necessary for some of the cooking procedures. In addition, it's helpful to have a double boiler for making some of the sauces and for melting chocolate.

Puréed soups are made creamy in a blender. I use a food processor for many procedures, such as chopping large quantities of onions, but I prefer cutting most vegetables on a generously sized cutting board with a sharp chef's knife. Use a whisk to ensure that your sauces will be smooth. You'll also need a set of bowls in various sizes. Handy tools include a vegetable peeler, a grater or microplane, a zester, basting brushes, tongs, measuring cups and spoons, a baking sheet and a jelly roll pan, a strainer, a colander, and a pepper mill. You'll notice that I've offered visual cues for determining when food is done, but it's also a good idea to count on a reliable timer to prevent overcooking. For making desserts, I recommend an electric mixer (a small hand mixer is fine) and a variety of baking pans, including a 9" pie plate.

The recipes deserve fine presentation, so I think it's important to have a variety of platters and serving dishes, both fancy and casual, to showcase your spirited creations.

USING THE *SPIRITED VEGETARIAN* RECIPES

Fresh ingredients are the stars of most of my recipes, and I suggest that you rely on garden-fresh seasonal produce whenever possible. But, for some recipes, certain ingredients, such as tomatoes and beans, are just fine from a can. And some vegetables, such as corn and peas, are acceptable in their frozen forms. I prefer using fresh herbs but have provided the conversion to dried herbs when they are an acceptable substitution in a recipe.

I've provided quantities for salt and pepper, followed by "or to taste," so sample the completed dish before adding any salt at all; then add it gradually. You'll find that salt suppresses the acidity of wine. Cheese garnishes, such as feta and Parmesan, add saltiness to a dish as it is served, so that has been considered in the amounts indicated as well. The type of vegetable stock used also will affect the amount of salt needed. In general, my preference is to use sea salt, which does not have the bitterness of table salt. Also, because it contains traces of many minerals, sea salt has a more complex flavor. I use regular sea salt for cooking and French *fleur de sel* for sprinkling on completed dishes (see Tips, page 125). If you prefer, you can use kosher salt, which has no additives, is less salty than table salt, and dissolves quickly.

Vegetable stock is an important ingredient many of the recipes in this book. Making it from scratch really isn't practical for most of us because of the time involved, so it's important to have good-quality packaged stock on hand. The choices are endless—liquid stock in cans or in aseptic boxes; cubes, granules, and concentrates to mix with water. In all types, the flavors differ significantly between brands. Some contain preservatives or sweeteners; some are very salty. Check the package labels and read the small print so you know what is in the product you select and how to store it. I suggest trying several to find the one you like best. I prefer using low-sodium stock, as well as unsalted butter, which allows me to better control the amount of salt and the final taste of the dish. This is especially important if you are reducing a sauce, which concentrates saltiness.

Many dishes call for Parmesan cheese, but in some recipes it may be grated and in others shredded. While these techniques could be considered inter-changeable, shredded and grated Parmesan cheese can offer a dish different mouth feels. Shredded Parmesan is cut into narrow strips. This can be done most easily using a food processor fitted with a shredding disk, or by hand using a medium-wide rasp microplane, a tool found in most gourmet shops. Grating involves cutting the cheese into small particles by rubbing it against a grater. I often use a handheld crank-type grater and a box grater, which collect the grated cheese in an attached container. These are sold at many gourmet shops.

You can vary the richness and calorie content of recipes by altering the dairy products, from heavy cream to fat-free milk and regular sour cream to fat-free sour cream.

Throughout the pages of this book, I've included tips on ingredients and pro-cedures, as well as kitchen wisdom. The tips are based on questions asked by my cooking class students, and I think they will be useful as you shop and prepare these recipes. On pages 20 and 21 is the list of Paulette's Tips, noting the pages where they appear.

I hope you'll find dishes here that you will return to time and time again. As you work with the recipes, I encourage you to make alterations and substitutions. Vary the beans. Use your favorite vegetables. And, of course, play with the wines and liqueurs to suit your mood, as well as what's in your refrigerator and liquor cabinet. Most important, have fun preparing these *spirited vegetarian* recipes as you create memorable meals to share with your family and guests.

Cheers!

Paulette's Tips

Appetizers and First Courses

Begin with a splash of spirits. Appetizers set the mood for a party—whether it is formal or casual, follows an ethnic theme, or celebrates a special event. The first dishes served must complement the following courses, especially the main course. Or, rather than a multicourse menu, you may want to serve simply an array of appetizers. These creations should be presented in a manner to reflect not only your theme but also your personality. Serve your *spirited vegetarian* appetizers with panache.

The recipes in this chapter are inspired by the world's cuisines. Some are light, others more substantial. Some are savory, such as Mixed Mushroom-Almond Pâté (*opposite page*), which is made with dry sherry, and rosemary-scented Olives Baked in Cabernet (*page 26*). One of my sweet and fruity favorites, Dried Fruit Compote with Chèvre (*page 30*), is made with a dessert-style wine. Several, including the Diced Vegetables in Endive Leaves with Sherried Plum Sauce (*page 28*) and the Zucchini Pancakes (*page 32*) with Fresh Herb Cream Sauce (*page 33*), can be served either as an appetizer or as a first course after your guests are seated at the table.

I've also offered instructions for making Bruschetta (*page 38*) and suggestions for embellishing those tasty Italian toasts with toppings and sauces that appear in other chapters.

In addition to the recipes in this chapter, several recipes in the Main Courses chapter make lovely appetizers or first courses when served in smaller portions. These include Polenta Triangles (*page 120*) with the various suggested sauces and toppings, Polenta Pizza (*page 122*), Roasted Vegetables (*page 123*), Tomato Pie (*page 126*), Red Wine Ratatouille (*page 134*), Carrot Patties with Orange-Sherry Sauce (*page 160*), and Vegetable Frittata (*page 164*) with your choice of sauce.

I'm a firm believer in enjoying my own parties, so most of these appetizers can be prepared in advance, requiring only a few minutes away from your guests just before serving. ❧

Mixed Mushroom-Almond Pâté

This smooth pâté is one of my favorite appetizers. It spreads nicely on wedges of pita or thick slices of a crusty baguette. French cornichons make a zesty accompaniment.

MAKES 1 CUP | VEGAN RECIPE

2	tablespoons olive oil	1	tablespoon minced fresh tarragon or $\frac{1}{2}$ teaspoon dried tarragon
1	cup sliced cremini mushrooms (about 3 ounces)	$\frac{1}{2}$	cup toasted slivered almonds (see Tips, page 73)
1	cup sliced oyster mushroom caps (about 3 ounces)	1	tablespoon fresh lemon juice
$\frac{1}{2}$	cup stemmed and sliced shiitake mushrooms	$\frac{1}{4}$	teaspoon salt, or to taste
$\frac{1}{2}$	cup coarsely chopped onion	$\frac{1}{4}$	teaspoon freshly ground pepper, or to taste
2	cloves garlic, minced		Red bell pepper strips, toasted slivered almonds, and sprigs of fresh flat-leaf parsley for garnish
$\frac{1}{4}$	cup dry sherry		

Heat the oil in a large skillet over medium heat. Add the mushrooms and onion and cook, stirring occasionally, until the mushrooms are tender, about 8 minutes. Add the garlic and stir constantly for about 1 minute. Add the sherry. Use a wooden spoon to stir, scraping up the browned juices from the bottom of the pan. Remove the pan from the heat, stir in the tarragon, and let cool.

Transfer the mushroom mixture to a food processor. Add the remaining ingredients, except the garnish, and process until smooth. Taste and adjust the seasoning.

Spoon the pâté into a bowl. Let stand for at least 1 hour or refrigerate in a covered container for up to 1 week before serving.

To serve, let the pâté come to room temperature. Garnish with bell pepper, almonds, and parsley sprigs.

Olives Baked in Cabernet

Black olives are quick to absorb the full-bodied flavors of wine and rosemary that lend character to this appetizer. It makes a great accompaniment to the Italian-inspired dishes I love so well. If you prefer the flavor of a lighter-bodied wine, substitute a dry rosé or Beaujolais.

MAKES ½ CUP | VEGAN RECIPE

½	cup pitted kalamata olives (see Tips)	2	cloves garlic, thinly sliced
¼	cup Cabernet Sauvignon or other full-bodied red wine	2	sprigs fresh rosemary, divided
		1	teaspoon extra-virgin olive oil

Preheat the oven to 325°F.

Combine the olives, wine, garlic, 1 rosemary sprig, and the olive oil in a small (about 2-cup) baking dish. Bake, uncovered, for about 20 minutes, or until the olives are thoroughly heated. Cool slightly, then remove and discard the rosemary sprig.

Transfer the olives and wine mixture to a small bowl. Serve warm or at room temperature garnished with the remaining rosemary sprig.

Refrigerate the olives in the wine mixture for up to 1 week in a covered glass container.

TIPS | *❧ Kalamata olives are eggplant-colored, almond-shaped olives from Greece, ranging from about ½" to 1" in length. These rich, fruity-flavored olives come packed in olive oil, brine, or wine vinegar, often slit open to allow the marinade in which they are soaking to be absorbed into the flesh. You'll find kalamata olives in supermarket olive bars and among the jarred olives. To extend the life of olives, store them in the refrigerator; for the best flavor, bring to room temperature before serving.*

Peppery Plum Chutney

I love the interplay of sweet-hot flavors that adds dimension to this chutney. Serve it atop small squares of a firm cheese, such as Spanish manchego, or with water crackers. The chutney will keep for up to 2 weeks in a tightly closed container in the refrigerator, ready for impromptu guests. If you prefer to accent the peppery quality further, make this chutney with Syrah rather than Merlot.

MAKES ABOUT ¾ CUP | VEGAN RECIPE (*if served without cheese*)

¼	cup finely chopped prunes	¼	teaspoon coarsely ground pepper
¼	cup finely chopped shallots	¼	teaspoon salt
¼	cup Merlot or other full-bodied, plummy red wine	1	sprig fresh thyme
¼	cup red wine vinegar	1	fresh, ripe, medium-size plum, pitted and finely chopped (see Tips)
1	tablespoon packed brown sugar		

Combine all the ingredients, except the fresh plum, in a small saucepan. Cover and bring to a boil over medium-high heat. Reduce the heat to low and simmer, stirring occasionally, until the prunes are soft and the liquid has thickened, about 5 minutes.

Add the fresh plum and continue to cook for 5 minutes. Remove and discard the thyme.

Transfer the mixture to a large bowl and let cool. Store in a tightly closed glass container in the refrigerator.

TIPS | ✿ *The many varieties of colorful plums range from yellow and green to red, purple, or black and from tiny as olives to large as a peach. Plums are in season from May to October. Store them at room temperature until they are slightly soft, then refrigerate in a plastic bag for up to 5 days. Plums don't require peeling, but wash them thoroughly before using.*

Diced Vegetables in Endive Leaves with Sherried Plum Sauce

The licorice tones of Chinese five-spice powder give this appetizer its special character. If you prefer to make the servings less substantial, fill the small inner endive leaves with just 1 tablespoon of the vegetables. Or, to make this into a light main course, chop the vegetables more coarsely, mound heaping quarter-cupfuls onto 6 baby romaine leaves, and pair the creation with Riesling.

Makes 6 servings (*2 filled leaves per serving*) | Vegan recipe

For the sauce

¼	cup store-bought Chinese plum sauce	2	tablespoons dry sherry

For the endive and vegetables

12	endive leaves, ends trimmed (see Tips)	3	ribs bok choy, cut into ¼" dice; also cut the green tops into a chiffonade (see Tips, page 157)
2	tablespoons dry sherry	2	carrots, cut into ¼" dice
2	tablespoons soy sauce	½	red bell pepper, finely chopped
1	tablespoon fresh lime juice	¼	yellow bell pepper, finely chopped
1	tablespoon finely chopped fresh cilantro	2	scallions, both white and green parts, minced
½	teaspoon Chinese five-spice powder (see Tips)	2	cloves garlic, minced
⅛	teaspoon ground white pepper, or to taste		Dash of salt, or to taste
	Pinch of red-pepper flakes, or to taste		Toasted sesame seeds (see Tips, page 133) or black sesame seeds for garnish
1	tablespoon peanut oil (preferably roasted peanut oil)		

To make the sauce, pour the plum sauce into a small bowl. Stir in the sherry and add water until the sauce is a maple-syrup consistency. Set aside.

To make the endive and vegetables, arrange the endive leaves on a platter. Stir together the sherry, soy sauce, lime juice, cilantro, five-spice powder, white pepper, and red-pepper flakes in a small bowl. Set aside.

Heat the oil in a large skillet or wok, over medium-high heat. Add the bok choy, carrots, bell peppers, and scallions. Cook, stirring constantly, until crisp-tender, about 5 minutes. Add the garlic and stir constantly for about 1 minute. Remove from the heat and stir in the soy sauce mixture. Taste and season with salt, as desired.

Serve the vegetables warm or let them come to room temperature. Fill each endive leaf with 2 heaping tablespoons of the vegetables, drizzle with about ½ tablespoon of the plum sauce, and sprinkle with sesame seeds.

TIPS | *Belgian endive is a member of the chicory family. The cone-shaped, slightly bitter-tasting salad green has slender, tightly packed 5" to 6" leaves. Their creamy appearance, marked by pale yellow tips, is the result of being grown in complete darkness to prevent them from turning green. To store Belgian endive, wrap it in a paper towel, place it in a plastic bag, and refrigerate for up to 2 days.*

Five-spice powder, sometimes called five-fragrance powder, is a sweet and pungent spice blend. The mixture, which varies depending on the supplier, generally is made with star anise, cinnamon, cloves, Szechuan peppercorns, and fennel seeds, which offer the predominant licorice flavor. Five-spice powder is available in Asian markets and among the Asian foods in most supermarkets.

DRIED FRUIT COMPOTE WITH CHÈVRE

Many thanks to Michael Hochhalter, a friend and cheese expert who shared this splendid recipe. Michael's trick is to enrich the fruit mixture with sweet wine and herbs, then mound it over a round of fresh chèvre. Pass thin slices of French baguette or flatbread crackers and serve with a semisweet or sweet sparkling wine, such as Prosecco. No need to follow the fruit quantities or choices exactly; use about 1½ cups total fruit, noting that a colorful variety will make the most stunning presentation.

MAKES 1½ CUPS | VEGAN RECIPE (*if compote is served without cheese*)

½ cup Sauterne or other dessert-style white wine

¼ cup golden raisins (see Tips)

¼ cup dried blueberries

¼ cup dried cranberries

¼ cup finely chopped dried dates

¼ cup finely chopped dried figs

¼ cup finely chopped dried apricots

Thin zest strips from 1 lemon

¼ cup fresh lemon juice

3 tablespoons extra-virgin olive oil

1 tablespoon honey

2 teaspoons finely chopped fresh thyme

2 scallions, both white and green parts, minced (see Tips)

6–8 ounces fresh white goat cheese (chèvre)

Toasted pine nuts (see Tips, page 73) and sprigs of fresh thyme for garnish

Bring the wine to a simmer in a small saucepan. Remove from the heat. Add the raisins, blueberries, cranberries, dates, figs, and apricots. Cover and let stand until the fruit is softened, about 30 minutes.

Meanwhile, whisk together the remaining ingredients, except the scallions and chèvre.

When the fruit has softened, stir in the scallions and the lemon juice mixture.

Transfer the fruit compote to a covered container (preferably glass) and refrigerate for up to 2 weeks. Stir before using.

To serve, form the chèvre into a 1"- to 1½"-thick round. Place the cheese on a platter. Top and surround it with the fruit compote and its juices. Garnish with pine nuts and thyme sprigs. Serve with a basket of bread or crackers. Provide cheese spreaders and small spoons for serving.

TIPS | ❧ *Dried fruits can be stored tightly wrapped at room temperature for up to 3 months. To store for up to 1 year, refrigerate in a tightly sealed plastic bag. When preparing a dish like this compote, it's easiest to chop dried fruits into uniform pieces using kitchen scissors rather than a knife. To prevent sticking, dip the scissors in hot water as needed.*

❧ *Scallions, also called green onions, are delicate members of the onion family that vary in size from very slender to thick; as a rule, the thicker the onion, the sweeter the flavor. Wrap unwashed scallions in a plastic bag and store them for up to 1 week in the vegetable-crisper drawer of the refrigerator.*

ZUCCHINI PANCAKES

Warning: These savory little pancakes have a way of disappearing fast! As a taste-tempting appetizer or first course, serve them with Fresh Herb Cream Sauce (opposite page), Tomato-Caper Sauce (page 34), Roasted Red Bell Pepper Sauce (page 170), or Spicy Merlot Marinara (page 168). The pancakes should be served warm. Keep them on a foil-covered plate in a 350°F oven for up to 15 minutes before serving. Or make them in advance and quickly reheat them in the microwave oven.

MAKES 16 (*4 servings*)

2	eggs
2	cups finely shredded zucchini
¼	cup finely chopped onion
¼	cup freshly grated Parmesan cheese
½	cup all-purpose flour
2	teaspoons finely chopped fresh oregano or ½ teaspoon dried oregano
½	teaspoon salt
¼	teaspoon ground white pepper
2	tablespoons olive oil

Lightly beat the eggs in a medium bowl. Stir in the zucchini, onion, and Parmesan.

In a small bowl, stir together the flour, oregano, salt, and pepper. Stir into the zucchini mixture.

Heat the oil in a large skillet over medium-high heat. Drop in heaping tablespoonfuls of the pancake mixture and flatten them with the back of a spoon. Cook until lightly browned on both sides and done all the way through, about 3 minutes per side.

As the pancakes are done, transfer them to a foil-covered plate.

Serve with your choice of sauce in a bowl on the side for your guests to drizzle over the pancakes.

Fresh Herb Cream Sauce

Hazelnut liqueur adds a surprise element to this richly flavored sauce. I'm especially fond of pairing it with Zucchini Pancakes (opposite page) to dress up the dish for company. Fresh herbs are a must here. And when I serve this sauce, a bottle of oaky Chardonnay is always on the table.

MAKES ½ CUP

1	cup Chardonnay or other rich, full-bodied white wine	1	teaspoon finely chopped fresh tarragon
2	tablespoons hazelnut liqueur, such as Frangelico	⅛	teaspoon salt, or to taste
1	small leek, white part only, quartered lengthwise and very thinly sliced (see Tips, page 61)	⅛	teaspoon ground white pepper, or to taste
2	teaspoons finely chopped fresh rosemary	½	cup half-and-half

Combine the wine and liqueur in a medium saucepan and bring to a boil over high heat. Reduce the heat to low and simmer, uncovered, until reduced to ½ cup, about 10 minutes.

Add the leek, rosemary, tarragon, salt, and pepper. Continue to simmer, uncovered, for 5 more minutes.

Add the half-and-half and simmer, whisking constantly to prevent curdling, until the sauce is slightly thickened, about 5 more minutes. Taste and adjust the seasoning.

Tomato-Caper Sauce

The addition of Pinot Noir adds elegance to this easy-to-prepare sauce. For an impressive first course or appetizer, serve it over Zucchini Pancakes (page 32), thin wedges of Vegetable Frittata (page 164), or small squares of polenta (page 120).

MAKES 1 CUP | VEGAN RECIPE

1	tablespoon olive oil
¼	cup finely chopped onion
1	clove garlic, minced
2	tomatoes, cut into ½" cubes
2	tablespoons Pinot Noir or other medium-bodied, earthy red wine
2	teaspoons finely chopped fresh oregano or ½ teaspoon dried oregano
1	tablespoon capers, drained and rinsed (see Tips)
¼	teaspoon salt, or to taste
¼	teaspoon freshly ground pepper, or to taste

Heat the oil in a medium saucepan over medium heat. Add the onion and cook, stirring occasionally, until translucent, about 5 minutes. Add the garlic and stir constantly for about 1 minute.

Stir in the remaining ingredients. Increase the heat to medium-high and bring to a boil.

Reduce the heat to low and simmer, uncovered, stirring occasionally until thickened, about 15 minutes. Taste and adjust the seasoning.

TIPS | ❧ *Capers are the flower buds of a shrub that grows in the Mediterranean and in parts of Asia. After drying in the sun, the buds are pickled in vinegar brine or packed in oil or coarse salt. Capers come in several sizes; the largest have the strongest flavor. The smallest, called "nonpareil," are subtler in taste, the most tender, and the most expensive. Rinse capers in cold running water before using to remove excess salt. Once the jar is opened, store capers in the refrigerator for up to 6 months.*

Cheese Fondue with Basil Pesto

When cooking with cheese, it's important to melt it over low heat to avoid a stringy or grainy texture. Adding an acidic ingredient, such as wine, also will help keep the cheese from separating. If you don't have fresh basil to make the pesto called for in this recipe, it's okay to purchase it from a gourmet shop or supermarket.

Makes 1 cup (*4 servings*)

¾ cup (3 ounces) finely shredded fontina cheese, at room temperature

¾ cup (3 ounces) finely shredded Swiss cheese, at room temperature

½ cup finely shredded Romano cheese, at room temperature

1 tablespoon all-purpose flour

1 clove garlic, halved

½ cup Sauvignon Blanc or other medium-bodied, high-acid white wine

1 tablespoon Kirsch

2 tablespoons Basil Pesto (*page 36*)

Water or milk, as needed

Bite-size chunks of French bread or breadsticks and vegetables, such as blanched broccoli and cauliflower florets, and cherry tomatoes for dipping

Toss together the 3 cheeses and the flour in a medium bowl.

Rub the garlic on the bottom and sides of a 1½-quart nonstick saucepan. Add the wine and warm over medium heat just until small bubbles rise to the surface. Reduce the heat to low. Add the cheese mixture about ½ cup at a time, stirring constantly. Make certain each addition melts before adding more. Stir in the Kirsch.

In a small bowl, combine the pesto with a little water or milk until it reaches a cake-batter consistency.

Transfer the cheese mixture to a small earthenware fondue dish, and keep it warm over low heat. Spoon the pesto in a spiral pattern over the top.

Serve with bowls or platters of the foods for dipping.

Basil Pesto

Hooked on its flavor and versatility, I always have pesto on hand. At the end of the growing season, I pinch the leaves from my basil plants and make plenty of the aromatic blend, some to use immediately and some to store in the freezer. For variety, sometimes I substitute shelled pistachios for the pine nuts. I like to swirl this fragrant paste into cheese fondue (page 35) and tomato soup (page 66), or spread it on bruschetta (page 38).

Makes ½ cup

1	cup loosely packed fresh basil leaves	2	tablespoons freshly grated Parmesan cheese
¼	cup extra-virgin olive oil (see Tips)	2	cloves garlic, minced
¼	cup pine nuts, preferably toasted (see Tips, page 73)	⅛	teaspoon salt, or to taste
		⅛	teaspoon freshly ground pepper, or to taste

Process all the ingredients in a food processor or blender until the mixture is a coarse purée. Using a rubber spatula, scrape down the sides as needed. Taste and adjust the seasoning.

Note: This pesto will keep for up to 1 week in a covered container in the refrigerator. Pour a thin film of olive oil on top of the pesto to prevent discoloration. For longer storage, omit the Parmesan when making the pesto. Spoon the mixture into an aluminum foil–lined custard cup, then cover tightly with foil and freeze. Once the pesto is frozen, remove the foil-wrapped packet and store it in a freezer bag for up to 2 months. Stir in the Parmesan after thawing.

TIPS | ❧ *When shopping for olive oil, you'll usually find 3 main choices: extra-virgin, regular, and light.*

Extra-virgin olive oil, the highest, most flavorful, and most expensive grade, is made from the first pressing of top-quality olives. It has a complex, full-bodied, fruity taste and low acidity. This makes it the best choice for uncooked dishes or for adding flavor in the final stages of cooking.

Olive oil, sometimes called pure olive oil, usually comes from refined oil that doesn't meet the criteria to become extra-virgin. (The refining process removes some of the color and flavor.) It's a good choice for cooking because the flavor of extra-virgin oil dissipates somewhat when heated.

Light olive oil has a lighter, less pronounced olive oil flavor and aroma, but it contains exactly the same amount of fat and calories.

The many varieties of olives, soils, and climates account for the many flavor differences among oils. Color can vary from light yellow to bright green—the deeper the color, the more intense the olive flavor.

Store all olive oils in a cool, dark place, and use within 6 months. Refrigerated, olive oil will keep for up to 1 year; although the oil will become thick and cloudy, this does not affect the flavor or quality. Simply bring it to room temperature before using to restore the clarity and liquid consistency. Once the oil smells rancid or tastes "off," it should be discarded.

BRUSCHETTA

Bruschetta is a traditional Italian garlic bread. These days, every Italian trattoria and many American restaurants offer their own versions.

To make Bruschetta, cut a French baguette or rustic Italian bread (day-old, if you like) into ½" to ¾"-thick slices. Toast the bread slices under the oven broiler, in a 400°F oven, or over a charcoal fire until golden brown and crisp on the outside, yet still chewy and not dry on the inside. If you are using the oven, arrange the bread slices in a single layer on a baking sheet. Toast the bread for 2 to 3 minutes on each side. Toast for less time under a broiler and over a charcoal fire. Watch closely so the bread does not burn.

Like the Italians, you can rub 1 side of each warm slice with cut garlic cloves; the more you rub, the stronger the flavor.

The toasts, which can be served as appetizers or as accompaniments to soups and salads, are a blank canvas that you can embellish with innumerable other fragrant and colorful toppings. The most simple is to drizzle the toasted and garlic-scented bread with extra-virgin olive oil and sprinkle with salt and pepper.

If you wish, toast the bread early in the day and complete your creations just before serving. Toppings that don't require heating can be spooned into a bowl to accompany a basket of the toasts. Your guests can assemble their own at the table.

In addition to the recipe for **Sun-Dried Tomato and Goat Cheese Bruschetta** (*page 40*), here are some suggested toppings:

🌿 Spread with Mixed Mushroom-Almond Pâté (*page 25*). Top with strips of roasted red bell peppers.

🌿 Spread with Basil Pesto (*page 36*). Top with thin slices of plum tomatoes, and sprinkle with salt, pepper, and freshly grated Parmesan cheese. Broil until the cheese melts.

🌿 Spread with a layer of fresh white goat cheese (chèvre), add thin slices of Pears Poached in Crème de Cassis (*page 87*), and top with slivers of pecorino Romano cheese.

🌿 Spread with pasta toppings, such as Triple-Tomato Pesto (*page 148*) or Spicy Merlot Marinara (*page 168*). (This is a great use for leftover sauce when it has thickened after setting.) Be creative. You can first spread the toasts with Basil Pesto (*page 36*) or fresh white goat cheese (chèvre). Top your creations with strips of Ruby Port–Glazed Portobello Mushrooms (*page 124*), olives, fresh herbs, or cheese.

Sun-Dried Tomato
and Goat Cheese Bruschetta

Goat cheese not only adds its signature piquancy, but it also prevents the bread from becoming soggy, allowing you to assemble this appetizer up to 1 hour in advance. Just before serving, broil to melt the Parmesan cheese.

Makes about 4 servings

1	tablespoon olive oil	1	tablespoon finely chopped fresh basil
¼	cup finely chopped onion		
2	cloves garlic, minced	⅛	teaspoon freshly ground pepper, or to taste
½	cup finely chopped oil-packed sun-dried tomatoes, drained well	12	slices Bruschetta (*page 38*) made using a thin French baguette
¼	cup Sangiovese or other medium-bodied, high-acid red wine	¼	cup fresh white goat cheese (chèvre), see Tips
2	tablespoons finely chopped kalamata olives	2	tablespoons freshly shredded Parmesan cheese

Position the oven broiler rack about 5" from the heating element. Preheat the broiler.

Heat the oil in a small sauté pan over medium heat. Add the onion and cook, stirring occasionally, until translucent, about 5 minutes. Add the garlic and stir constantly for about 1 minute. Stir in the tomatoes and wine. Reduce the heat to low and simmer, uncovered, until the liquid evaporates, about 5 minutes. Remove the pan from the heat. Let cool. Stir in the olives, basil, and pepper. Taste and adjust the seasoning.

Arrange the bruschetta on a baking sheet. Spread each with about 1 teaspoon of the chèvre. Top with about 1 tablespoon of the tomato mixture and sprinkle with about ½ teaspoon of the Parmesan.

Broil for about 30 seconds, or until the cheese is melted. Serve warm or at room temperature.

TIPS | ❊ **Chèvre** *is the French name for a tart, soft cheese made from goat's milk. It's available both fresh and white or coated with herbs and pepper. Domestic goat cheese is a fine substitute for the more expensive imported brands. Once chèvre is opened, wrap it tightly in plastic and store it in the refrigerator for up to 2 weeks. If the flavor turns sour, the cheese should be discarded. Do not confuse fresh white goat cheese with feta cheese or caprini—Italian goat cheese—which is aged, less creamy, and more acidic.*

❊ *After purchasing, fresh and soft-ripened cheeses should be tightly wrapped; they will keep in the coldest part of the refrigerator for up to 2 weeks. Discard fresh or soft-ripened cheeses that become moldy.*

Any firm, semifirm, or semisoft cheese should be wrapped airtight in a plastic bag or foil. After using, discard the wrapping and rewrap freshly. Store in your refrigerator's cheese compartment (or warmest location) for up to several weeks. Mold may be cut away if it develops.

Cheese served directly from the refrigerator will never have the full, rich flavor of cheese at room temperature. Before serving or melting, let the cheese come to room temperature while still in the wrapping (about 30 to 60 minutes), so the cut surfaces will not dry out.

RED WINE JELLY

This is a great way to use the last of a bottle of wine, and it's a lovely gift from your kitchen to share with friends. My friend Fran, who makes jams and jellies galore, says it's unnecessary to cover them in the traditional manner using paraffin. Instead, store the jelly in a tightly covered jar in the refrigerator for up to 3 weeks or in the freezer for up to 1 year.

As an appetizer, I love to top thin slices of French baguette with a sliver of Gruyère and a dollop of this jelly to savor the contrast of sweet and salty. Or, I simply spread the jelly on thin slices of French bread, perhaps over a layer of chèvre, to accompany salads.

For dessert, use wine jelly as a glaze for a fruit tart or cake; melt the jelly over low heat, spread it with a brush, and then chill the creation.

MAKES 3½ CUPS | VEGAN RECIPE

3	cups sugar	3	ounces liquid fruit pectin (see Tips)
2	cups Red Zinfandel or other full-bodied, jammy red wine		

Combine the sugar and wine in the top pan of a double boiler over simmering water (see Tips, page 212). Stir constantly until the sugar dissolves, about 5 minutes. Add the pectin and stir constantly for about 1 minute. Use a large spoon to skim off the foam.

While the jelly is still hot, pour it into hot, sterilized jars (see Tips). Leave a ½" space at the top for expansion if you choose to freeze the jelly. Wipe the rims clean and tightly screw on the lids. Let stand at room temperature for 24 hours or until set, then transfer to the refrigerator or freezer.

TIPS | ❧ *Pectin, a natural substance derived from fruits, is used for thickening jellies, jams, and preserves. Liquid pectin, which comes from apples, thickens properly only when mixed with the correct balance of sugar and acid.*

❧ *To sterilize glass jars, first wash and rinse them. Then immerse in boiling water for at least 10 minutes, or until needed.*

CRANBERRY MARGARITA RELISH

*Using a food processor, this crunchy, fresh relish takes just minutes to prepare. It can be served right away but is best if it stands for at least 30 minutes to allow the flavors to marry. It stores well in the refrigerator for up to 1 week. As an appetizer, serve the relish on crackers spread with chèvre or in endive leaves with a dollop of crème fraiche. The relish also makes a fine accompaniment to **Ruby Port-Glazed Portobello Mushrooms** (page 124), as a vibrant accent to a festive meal.*

MAKES 3 CUPS

4	cups (14 ounces) fresh cranberries or frozen unsweetened cranberries, thawed (see Tips)	½	cup sugar
		3	tablespoons orange-flavored liqueur, such as Cointreau
1	teaspoon orange zest	1	tablespoon tequila
2	large seedless oranges, peeled and coarsely chopped	1	tablespoon fresh lime juice

Combine the cranberries, orange zest, oranges, and sugar in a food processor. Process until the mixture is chunky. Stir in the liqueur, tequila, and lime juice.

Transfer to a covered container and refrigerate.

TIPS | ❧ *Cranberries, which are grown in northern parts of North America, are available fresh from October through November. Tightly wrapped and refrigerated, they will keep for up to 2 months or can be frozen for up to 1 year. Because of their tartness, cranberries are best when combined with other fruits.*

Soups and Stews

During any season, soup will raise your spirits. Tureens of hearty, piping hot soup warm us when the winter winds blow, and chilled soup brings refreshment on a steamy summer day. Soup-making is often inspired by a trip to the farmers' market or by the vegetables or beans you have on hand. The task is simple and can be done in advance. For both easygoing and elegant entertaining, soup provides wonderful possibilities, and the recipes can easily be multiplied to serve a crowd. Soups and stews can make a meal in themselves. Pair with a salad and artisan bread for a satisfying do-ahead family supper or a casually sophisticated meal for guests.

Spirits import body, color, flavor, and incomparable aroma to these soups. You may be familiar with adding dry sherry to soups; feel free to substitute a medium-dry, sweeter sherry. Here you'll also discover that Syrah lends its enticing peppery qualities to **Mediterranean Bean Stew** (*page 50*), Merlot contributes its plummy character to lentils, Riesling blends beautifully with miso, and Cognac makes the **Roasted Butternut Squash and Pear Bisque** (*page 72*) memorable.

Another important ingredient in meatless soups is vegetable stock. See page 18 for an explanation of various types and how they'll affect your soup.

Some of the *spirited vegetarian* soups in this chapter are bursting with large chunks of vegetables and beans. Others are velvet-smooth. **Fennel and Vegetable Soup with Sherried Mushrooms** (*page 64*), **Fresh Pea Soup with Gremolata** (*page 76*), and **Roasted Tomato Soup with Basil Pesto** (*page 66*) offer a rich flavor without the need for cream. The secret is to cook the vegetables until very tender. I've found that a blender breaks down the fibers more efficiently than a food processor and yields a smoother consistency.

To ensure safe blending, follow these steps: After cooking, let the vegetables and stock cool for 5 to 10 minutes. Purée in several batches, filling the blender container only up to one-half full and holding a towel over the lid. Start with the lowest speed and pulse, then gradually increase the speed until the soup is smooth. You'll need a bowl to hold the puréed mixture before it is poured back into the pot, which should be rinsed out before you return the soup to it for re-heating. Alternatively, you can use a handheld blender, also called an immersion blender, which you can lower directly into the pot of soup.

I like my creamy soups quite thick, but you can adjust the consistency by adding more milk, vegetable stock, or water. Adding more wine is likely to make the flavor too strong.

Another pleasure of soups: They can be made in advance and reheat well. In fact, the flavors often improve. Many soups thicken over time, so it may be necessary to thin them with stock, water, or milk when reheating.

Try the 2 chilled soups when it's just too hot to face the stove. They make a lovely addition to brunch and a surprising way to serve an effervescent wine. ❧

Sweet Potato Stew

I love the flavor of sweet potatoes, and here's one of my favorite ways to enjoy their beta-carotene benefits. Cornbread and a red wine, such as an aromatic and fruity Côtes du Rhône, complement their earthy flavor and brilliant color. It's the perfect combination for a winter feast.

MAKES 8 CUPS (*6 servings*) | VEGAN RECIPE

2	tablespoons olive oil	1	can (15 ounces) black beans, drained and rinsed
1	cup coarsely chopped onion	2	large tomatoes cut into ½" cubes
1	red bell pepper, coarsely chopped	½	cup coarsely chopped prunes
4	cloves garlic, minced	½	cup dry sherry
2	cups vegetable stock (see page 18)	¼	teaspoon salt, or to taste
2	medium orange-fleshed sweet potatoes (about 12 ounces each), peeled and cut into ½" cubes (see Tips)	¼	teaspoon freshly ground pepper, or to taste

Heat the oil in a Dutch oven over medium heat. Add the onion and bell pepper and cook, stirring occasionally, until the bell pepper is tender, about 8 minutes. Add the garlic and stir constantly for about 1 minute. Stir in the vegetable stock, sweet potatoes, beans, tomatoes, and prunes. Increase the heat to high and bring to a boil. Reduce the heat. Then stir in the sherry, cover, and simmer, stirring occasionally, until the potatoes are tender, about 20 minutes. Add the salt and pepper. Taste and adjust the seasoning.

TIPS | *❦ What is labeled a "yam" at the supermarket most likely is an orange sweet potato. It has a dark brown skin, a shape that tapers on both ends, bright orange flesh, and a sweet flavor when cooked. White sweet potatoes have a lighter, thinner skin; pale yellow flesh; and a less sweet flavor. Store sweet potatoes unwrapped in a cool, dry, dark, and well-ventilated place for up to 2 weeks. Do not refrigerate.*

Fava Bean Stew

To take the chill out of a winter night, here's a meal in a bowl, brimming with chunky vegetables, comforting potatoes, and hearty beans. Using canned beans makes this stew speedy to prepare and also eliminates the problem of tough bean skins, which is a concern when cooking dried beans from scratch with wine.

MAKES 8 CUPS (*6 servings*) | VEGAN RECIPE (*if feta cheese garnish is omitted*)

2	tablespoons olive oil	1	carrot, cut into 1/4"-thick slices
1/2	cup coarsely chopped onion	1	tablespoon finely chopped fresh oregano or 1 teaspoon dried oregano
4	cloves garlic, minced, divided		
1	can (28 ounces) plum tomatoes, halved	2	tablespoons tomato paste
1	can (19 ounces) fava beans, drained and rinsed (see Tips)	2	tablespoons finely chopped fresh flat-leaf parsley
1	cup vegetable stock (see page 18)	2	tablespoons finely chopped fresh basil
1/2	cup Pinot Grigio or other light-bodied, medium-acid white wine	1/2	teaspoon freshly ground pepper, or to taste
3	small red-skinned potatoes, scrubbed and cut into 1/2" cubes	1/4	teaspoon salt, or to taste
1	zucchini, halved lengthwise and cut into 1/4"-thick slices (see Tips)		Freshly ground pepper and crumbled feta cheese for garnish
1	cup green beans in 2" pieces		

Heat the oil in a Dutch oven over medium heat. Add the onion and cook, stirring occasionally, until translucent, about 5 minutes. Add 2 cloves of the garlic and stir constantly for about 1 minute.

Stir in the tomatoes (with juice), fava beans, vegetable stock, wine, potatoes, zucchini, green beans, carrot, and oregano. Increase the heat to high and bring to a boil. Reduce the heat to low, then cover and simmer, stirring occasionally, until the vegetables are tender, about 20 minutes.

Stir together the tomato paste, parsley, basil, pepper, salt, and the remaining 2 cloves of garlic in a small bowl. Add about ½ cup of the soup liquid and stir until smooth. Stir this mixture into the soup. Taste and adjust the seasoning.

Ladle into large bowls and garnish with pepper and feta cheese.

TIPS | ❧ *Fava beans (also called broad beans and horse beans) look like very large, dark-skinned lima beans. You can find fresh favas in supermarkets in the spring, still in their large, green pods (only about 4 to 6 to a pod), but you can also purchase them dried or in cans year-round. Fava beans are popular in Mediterranean and Middle Eastern dishes.*

❧ *Squash come in 2 distinct categories: summer squash and winter squash. Summer squash, including crookneck, pattypan, and zucchini, have thin, edible skins and soft seeds. For the best flavor, choose small to medium zucchini, about 6" long and up to 2" in diameter.*

MEDITERRANEAN BEAN STEW

This hearty stew is brimming with vegetables, pasta, and beans. The recipe multiplies easily to serve as dinner for a crowd. And yes, it's the answer to a host's prayer: You can make it ahead. After standing for a day or two, the liquid becomes absorbed in the pasta, so it may be necessary to thin the stew by adding vegetable stock or water. I like to serve this with a medium-bodied red wine, such as Pinot Noir or Côtes du Rhône.

MAKES 7 CUPS (*6 servings*) | **VEGAN RECIPE**
(*if Parmesan or feta cheese garnish is omitted*)

1	tablespoon olive oil		1	tablespoon finely chopped fresh oregano or 1/2 teaspoon dried oregano
1/2	cup finely chopped onion			
2	cloves garlic, minced		2	tablespoons finely chopped fresh basil or 1 teaspoon dried basil
1/2	cup Syrah or other full-bodied, peppery red wine			Pinch of red-pepper flakes, or to taste
3 1/2	cups vegetable stock (see page 18)		1	cup medium pasta shells
1	can (15 ounces) diced tomatoes		1/4	teaspoon salt, or to taste
1	can (19 ounces) cannellini beans, drained and rinsed		1/4	teaspoon freshly ground pepper, or to taste
2	cups green beans in 2" lengths			Thinly shaved Parmesan cheese or crumbled feta cheese for garnish
1	carrot, cut into 1/8"-thick slices			
2	tablespoons tomato paste (see Tips)			

Heat the oil in a Dutch oven over medium heat. Add the onion and cook, stirring occasionally, until translucent, about 5 minutes. Add the garlic and stir constantly for about 1 minute. Reduce the heat to low and add the wine. Use a wooden spoon to stir, scraping up the browned juices from the bottom of the pan.

Stir in the vegetable stock, tomatoes (with juice), cannellini beans, green beans, carrot, tomato paste, oregano, dried basil (if using), and red-pepper flakes. Increase the heat to high. When the liquid comes to a boil, stir in the pasta. Reduce the heat to medium, cover, and cook, stirring occasionally, until the vegetables and pasta are tender, about 8 minutes. Add the fresh basil (if using) during the last few minutes.

Stir in the salt and pepper. Taste and adjust the seasoning.

Garnish the servings with Parmesan or feta cheese.

TIPS | ❧ *Tomato paste is made from tomatoes that have been slowly cooked for hours until they are thick and concentrated in flavor.*

The paste is available in tubes—perfect for recipes calling for less than a 6-ounce can, as well as quick and simple to use. Refrigerate the tube for up to 6 months after opening.

CHILI WITH RAISINS

The smoky heat of chipotle chile peppers is balanced by the sweetness of the raisins. When you're feeling bold, add 2 chiles for more heat. Serve this with cornbread, a green salad, and perhaps a glass of bright and fruity Beaujolais Nouveau.

MAKES 6 CUPS (*4 servings*) | VEGAN RECIPE
(*if cheese and sour cream garnishes are omitted*)

1	small chipotle chile pepper (wear plastic gloves when handling), see Tips
2	tablespoons olive oil
1	cup coarsely chopped onion
1	green bell pepper, coarsely chopped
1	rib celery, coarsely chopped
4	cloves garlic, minced
1	tablespoon chili powder (see Tips)
1	teaspoon ground cumin
1	can (28 ounces) diced tomatoes
1	can (15 ounces) kidney beans, drained and rinsed
½	cup Syrah or other full-bodied, peppery red wine
½	cup dark raisins
2	tablespoons finely chopped fresh basil or 1 teaspoon dried basil
1	tablespoon finely chopped fresh oregano or 1 teaspoon dried oregano
¼	teaspoon salt, or to taste
¼	teaspoon freshly ground pepper, or to taste
	Shredded Cheddar cheese and sour cream for garnish

In a small bowl, cover the chile with very hot (not boiling) water to cover. Soak for about 15 to 20 minutes, or until the chile is soft. Remove and discard the stem and seeds and chop the chile finely.

Heat the oil in a Dutch oven over medium heat. Add the onion, bell pepper, and celery. Cook, stirring occasionally, until the bell pepper is tender, about 10 minutes. Add the garlic, chili powder, and ground cumin. Stir constantly for about 1 minute.

Stir in the tomatoes (with juice), beans, wine, raisins, dried basil (if using), oregano, and the chile. Increase the heat to high and bring to a boil. Reduce the heat to low, then cover and simmer, stirring occasionally, until the raisins are plumped, about 15 minutes. Stir in the fresh basil (if using), salt, and pepper. Taste and adjust the seasoning.

Garnish the servings with cheese and sour cream.

TIPS | ❧ *Chipotle chiles are dried and smoked jalapeño peppers. They have a wrinkled, dark brown skin and a smoky, sweet, medium-to-hot flavor. Select dried chiles that are slightly pliable; store them in an airtight container in a cool, dark place for up to 6 months. Before using, rinse under cool running water to remove any dust. Then cover with very hot (not boiling) water and soak for 15 to 20 minutes, or until softened. (Do not add the soaking water to recipes because it can be bitter.)*

As with fresh chiles, the seeds and the membranes contain most of the capsaicin—the compound that makes chiles fiery; removing the seeds and veins is the only way to reduce the heat. To avoid burns, use disposable plastic gloves when handling hydrated (or fresh) chiles. The easiest way to chop them is to use kitchen scissors; cut the seeded halves into strips, then snip across the strips to make small squares.

❧ *Chili powder is a blend of various ground, dried chile peppers with the addition of seasonings, such as garlic and onion powder. For more flavor, use pure chile powder, made only from dried, ground chile peppers. You can make your own by pulverizing dried chile skins (slice them open to remove the stems and seeds) in a clean coffee grinder. To retain the flavor and color, store chile powder in a tightly sealed jar in the refrigerator.*

CHUNKY BLACK BEAN SOUP

The bold flavors of this chunky soup become even more appealing with the addition of sherry. Add more red-pepper flakes if you'd like it even zestier. Serve with a sweet, fruity white wine, such as Gewürztraminer, or a jammy red, such as Shiraz or Red Zinfandel.

MAKES 5 CUPS (*4 servings*) | VEGAN RECIPE

2	tablespoons olive oil	½	cup dry sherry
1	cup finely chopped onion	1	can (15 ounces) black beans, drained and rinsed
2	carrots, finely chopped		
1	rib celery, finely chopped	¼	teaspoon freshly ground pepper, or to taste
4	cloves garlic, minced		
½	teaspoon ground cumin	⅛	teaspoon red-pepper flakes, or to taste
½	teaspoon ground coriander	¼	teaspoon salt, or to taste
3	cups vegetable stock (see page 18)		Sour cream and finely chopped red bell pepper for garnish

Heat the oil in a Dutch oven over medium heat. Add the onion, carrots, and celery. Cook, stirring occasionally, until the vegetables are crisp-tender, about 8 minutes. Add the garlic, cumin, and coriander and stir constantly for about 30 seconds. Stir in the remaining ingredients, except the salt and garnish. Increase the heat to high and bring to a boil. Reduce the heat, then cover and simmer until the vegetables are tender, about 20 minutes. Remove from the heat and let the soup cool for a few minutes.

Transfer 1 cup of the soup and beans to a blender and purée until smooth. Stir the puréed mixture into the soup and add the salt. Warm, stirring constantly, over medium heat. Taste and adjust the seasoning.

Garnish the servings with a dollop of sour cream topped with red bell pepper.

Curried Lentil Soup

I call this spirited vegetarian comfort food at its best! This robust soup is the perfect main course for a family dinner. Another cause for comfort: You can make it in advance, and the flavors will marry as the soup mellows in the refrigerator for a day or two. The lentils may absorb some of the liquid, so add water or vegetable stock when reheating.

Makes 8 cups (*8 servings*) | Vegan recipe

2	tablespoons olive oil	1	can (15 ounces) diced tomatoes
1	cup finely chopped red onion	½	cup Merlot or other full-bodied, plummy red wine
2	cloves garlic, minced		
2	tablespoons curry powder	¼	cup finely chopped fresh flat-leaf parsley
6	cups vegetable stock (see page 18)	¼	teaspoon salt, or to taste
1½	cups dried brown lentils	¼	teaspoon freshly ground pepper, or to taste
2	carrots, finely chopped		

Heat the oil in a Dutch oven over medium heat. Add the onion and cook, stirring occasionally, until translucent, about 5 minutes. Add the garlic and curry powder and stir constantly for about 30 seconds.

Stir in the vegetable stock, lentils, and carrots. Bring to a boil over high heat. Reduce the heat to low, then cover and simmer, stirring occasionally, until the lentils are tender, about 45 minutes.

Stir in the tomatoes (with juice), wine, parsley, salt, and pepper. Taste and adjust the seasoning.

Barley Soup with Miso

During my travels to Asia, I came to love miso for its wonderful salty depth, texture, and rich flavor. Combining it with Riesling's fruity character creates a uniquely flavorful vegetable-barley soup.

Makes 5 cups (*4 servings*) | **Vegan recipe**

⅓ cup barley (either regular or quick-cooking)

2 tablespoons canola oil

1½ cups finely chopped onion

3 cups sliced cremini mushrooms (about 8 ounces)

2 teaspoons minced fresh ginger

½ cup Riesling or other medium-bodied, high-acid, semisweet white wine

3½ cups hot water

¼ cup brown miso (see Tips)

2 carrots, finely chopped

½ teaspoon freshly ground pepper, or to taste

Minced scallions, green parts only, for garnish

Cook the barley according to the package instructions.

Meanwhile, heat the oil in a Dutch oven over medium heat. Add the onion and cook, stirring occasionally, until translucent, about 5 minutes. Add the mushrooms and ginger. Cook, stirring frequently, until the mushrooms are tender, about 5 minutes. Reduce the heat to low and add the wine. Use a wooden spoon to stir, scraping up the browned juices from the bottom of the pan.

Combine the hot water and miso in a small bowl. Whisk until the miso is dissolved. Add to the mushroom mixture. Stir in the carrots and the cooked barley. Increase the heat to high. Just before the soup comes to a boil, reduce the heat to low. Cover and simmer the soup until the carrots are tender, about 8 minutes. Stir in the pepper. Taste and adjust the seasoning.

Sprinkle the servings with scallions.

TIPS | ❧ *Miso, a Japanese condiment made from soybeans, is easily digested and highly nutritious, rich in B vitamins and protein. Look for it in Asian markets and in the refrigerated section of some supermarkets, where it is sold in vacuum-sealed pouches or tubs. There are 4 basic varieties of miso, each with a different color and flavor. In general, the darker the color, the stronger, saltier, and more robust the flavor. Store miso in the refrigerator for up to 1 year; it keeps well because of its high sodium content.*

Wild Mushroom Soup

Pinot Grigio, a light-bodied white wine, makes the perfect partner for this soup. I've often pre-
pared it simply with cremini mushrooms. But, to tell the truth, I enjoy it the most when I use a
variety of "wild" mushrooms (which are now cultivated), such as cremini, shiitake, chanterelle,
and oyster. Each offers a unique flavor and texture. At the supermarket, select the freshest-looking
mushrooms to create your own signature combination. See the Tips on page 151 for descriptions
of the characteristics of wild mushrooms and special considerations in selecting and using them.

MAKES 5 CUPS (*4 servings*) | VEGAN RECIPE

2	tablespoons olive oil, divided	3	tablespoons tomato paste
1	cup finely chopped onion	1	tablespoon finely chopped fresh oregano or 1 teaspoon dried oregano
3	cups sliced wild mushrooms (about 8 ounces), see Tips		
2	cloves garlic, minced	2	tablespoons finely chopped fresh flat-leaf parsley
½	cup Pinot Grigio or other light-bodied, medium-acid white wine	¼	teaspoon salt, or to taste
4	cups vegetable stock (see page 18)	¼	teaspoon freshly ground pepper, or to taste

Heat 1 tablespoon of the oil in a Dutch oven over medium heat. Add the onion
and cook, stirring occasionally, until translucent, about 5 minutes. Add the remaining 1 tablespoon of oil and stir in the mushrooms and garlic. Cook, stirring
occasionally, until the mushrooms are nearly tender, about 5 minutes.

Reduce the heat to medium-low and add the wine. Use a wooden spoon to stir,
scraping up the browned juices from the bottom of the pan.

Whisk together the vegetable stock, tomato paste, and oregano. Stir into the soup. Increase the heat to high and bring to a boil, then reduce the heat to low and simmer gently until the mushrooms are tender, about 15 minutes. Stir in the parsley, salt, and pepper. Taste and adjust the seasoning.

TIPS | ❧ *Keep mushrooms cool and dry. Refrigerate them in a basket or an open paper bag. Mushrooms stay firmer if there is air circulating around them so they can "breathe." Keep mushrooms away from strong-flavored foods because they will pick up odors. Avoid cleaning them until just before using.*

To clean mushrooms, trim the stems but do not soak them; mushrooms are like sponges and will absorb water and become mushy. Instead, wipe them with a damp cloth or paper towel, or use a mushroom brush. If necessary, rinse mushrooms briefly under cool running water and blot dry with paper towels.

Arborio Rice and Pumpkin Soup

The best pumpkins for cooking are sugar, or pie, pumpkins rather than jack-o'-lantern pumpkins, which are fibrous and flavorless. In place of the pumpkin, you can substitute any orange-fleshed winter squash. The flavor of either is enhanced by the addition of a fruity white wine.

MAKES 5 CUPS (*4 servings*) | VEGAN RECIPE (*if cheese garnish is omitted*)

2	tablespoons olive oil	2	cups peeled sugar pumpkin in ½" cubes (see note)
2½	cups sliced cremini mushrooms (about 7 ounces)	1	teaspoon finely chopped fresh rosemary or ½ teaspoon dried rosemary, crushed (see Tips)
2	leeks, white parts only, coarsely chopped (see Tips)	1	teaspoon orange zest
½	cup Gewürztraminer or other medium-bodied, sweet and fruity white wine	2	tablespoons fresh orange juice
		½	teaspoon salt, or to taste
½	cup Arborio rice	½	teaspoon freshly ground pepper, or to taste
3	cloves garlic, minced		
4	cups vegetable stock (see page 18)		Very thin slices of pecorino Romano cheese (see Tips) for garnish

Heat the oil in a Dutch oven over medium heat. Add the mushrooms and leeks and cook, stirring occasionally, until tender, about 5 minutes. Add the wine, rice, and garlic. Use a wooden spoon to stir, scraping up the browned juices from the bottom of the pan.

Stir in the vegetable stock, pumpkin, rosemary, and orange zest. Increase the heat to high and bring to a boil. Reduce the heat. Cover and simmer for about 15 minutes, or until the rice and pumpkin are tender. Stir in the orange juice, salt, and pepper. Taste and adjust the seasoning. Using a vegetable peeler, cut very thin slices of cheese to garnish the servings.

Note: For easy peeling, follow the procedure described in the squash tip on page 131.

TIPS | ❊ *Leeks, which look like giant scallions, are available year-round in most areas. Select those with crisp, bright green leaves and thin, unblemished white portions. Those less than 1¹/₂" in diameter will be the tenderest and most delicately flavored. Refrigerate them in a plastic bag for up to 5 days. Before using, trim the rootlets and leaf ends and slit the leeks from top to bottom. Wash thoroughly to remove the dirt and sand that is often trapped between the tight leaf layers. I find that the best method to do this is to chop the leeks first, and then immerse the pieces in a large bowl filled with cool water. As you swish the leeks with your hands, the loose dirt will settle at the bottom of the bowl. Remove the cleaned pieces with a slotted spoon or small strainer.*

❊ *Rosemary has a bold taste, so use it sparingly. To enhance the flavor and reduce the splintery texture of dried rosemary, crush the leaves between your fingers just before adding to a dish. When finely chopping fresh herbs that have twiglike stems, such as rosemary and thyme, use only the leaves and tender tips of the stems.*

❊ *Taking its name from the city of Rome, Romano cheese comes in several different styles. The best known is the firm, sharp, tangy imported pecorino Romano, which is made with sheep's milk. Most domestic Romanos are made of cow's milk, or a combination of cow's milk and goat's or sheep's milk.*

CARAMELIZED SWEET ONION SOUP WITH BUTTERED CROUTONS

Long ago, I learned that the secret to a good onion soup is cooking the onions slowly, allowing their rich flavors to develop and their sugars to caramelize. I like this recipe made with either a high-acid red or a white wine, each offering its hue and unique flavor. Both are scrumptious.

MAKES 4 CUPS (*4 servings*)

For the soup

4	tablespoons unsalted butter
1	pound sweet onions, such as Vidalia, quartered and thinly sliced (about 6 cups), see Tips, page 71
½	pound red onions, quartered and thinly sliced (about 3 cups)
½	cup thinly sliced shallots
4	cloves garlic, minced
¾	cup Sangiovese or Sauvignon Blanc or other high-acid red or white wine
3	cups vegetable stock (see page 18)
1	tablespoon finely chopped fresh thyme or 1 teaspoon dried thyme
¼	teaspoon salt, or to taste
¼	teaspoon freshly ground pepper, or to taste

For the croutons

4	thin slices of day-old white or whole-wheat bread
2	tablespoons freshly and finely grated Parmesan cheese
¼	teaspoon paprika, preferably Hungarian
⅛	teaspoon salt
2	tablespoons unsalted butter
2	tablespoons olive oil

To make the soup, melt the butter in a Dutch oven over medium heat. Add the onions and stir well to coat with the butter. Reduce the heat to medium-low. Cover and cook, stirring occasionally, until tender and golden brown, about 30 minutes. (Don't let the onions burn or they'll become bitter.)

Add the shallots and garlic and stir constantly for about 2 minutes. Add the wine. Use a wooden spoon to stir, scraping up the browned juices from the bottom of the pan. Continue to cook, uncovered, stirring constantly, until all the liquid is reduced and soaked into the onions, about 10 minutes.

Stir in the vegetable stock and thyme. Increase the heat and bring to a boil. Reduce the heat to medium-low, then cover and simmer, stirring occasionally, for about 20 minutes. Stir in the salt and pepper. Taste and adjust the seasoning.

Meanwhile, to make the croutons, use a round cookie cutter or an inverted glass to cut the bread into rounds smaller than the top of your soup bowls. (Avoid using the crust.)

Combine the Parmesan, paprika, and salt in a small brown paper bag or plastic container with a lid. Set aside.

Melt the butter with the oil in a large skillet over medium-high heat. When the mixture is so hot that drops of water sizzle when sprinkled into the pan, add the bread rounds. Cook, using tongs to turn, until lightly browned on the outside, yet still pliable, about 3 to 4 minutes per side.

While the croutons are still hot, drop them, one at a time, into the paper bag or plastic container containing the Parmesan mixture. Close or cover the container and shake until the croutons are lightly coated. Transfer to a plate to cool.

To serve, ladle the soup into bowls and float 1 crouton on top of each serving.

Fennel and Vegetable Soup with Sherried Mushrooms

Rich in looks, rich in taste, but not in fat. The secret: This full-bodied soup is thickened with cooked winter vegetables, not cream. The sherried mushrooms add a touch of elegance; for color and texture, adorn each serving with feathery fennel greens.

The soup can be made in advance and stored in a covered container in the refrigerator; the mushrooms are best when cooked just before serving. Don't be put off by the long ingredient list. The soup and mushrooms are very simple to prepare.

Makes 7 cups (*6 servings*) | **Vegan recipe**
(*if made with vegetable oil instead of butter*)

2	tablespoons unsalted butter		2	bay leaves
1½	cups fresh or frozen corn		2	tablespoons olive oil
1	medium, orange-fleshed sweet potato (about 10 ounces), peeled and cut into ½" cubes		3	cups sliced cremini mushrooms (about 8 ounces)
1	medium russet potato, peeled and cut into ½" cubes		2	cloves garlic, minced
2	ribs celery and leaves, coarsely chopped		1	tablespoon dry sherry
1	carrot, coarsely chopped		1	teaspoon fresh lemon juice
½	cup coarsely chopped onion		¾	teaspoon sweet paprika
1	fennel bulb, quartered and thinly sliced (see Tips, page 67)		2	tablespoons finely chopped fresh flat-leaf parsley
6	cups vegetable stock (see page 18)			Dash of salt + ¼ teaspoon, or to taste
¼	cup dry sherry			Dash of freshly ground pepper + ¼ teaspoon, or to taste
1	tablespoon finely chopped fresh thyme or 1 teaspoon dried thyme			Freshly ground pepper, mushrooms, and sprigs of fennel greens for garnish

Melt the butter in a Dutch oven over medium heat. Add the corn, potatoes, celery, carrot, onion, and fennel. Cook, stirring occasionally, until the vegetables are crisp-tender, about 10 minutes.

Stir in the vegetable stock, sherry, thyme, and bay leaves. Increase the heat to high and bring to a boil. Reduce the heat, then cover and simmer until the vegetables are very tender, about 20 minutes.

Heat the oil in a medium skillet over medium heat while the soup is cooking. Add the mushrooms and garlic to the oil and cook, stirring occasionally, until the mushrooms are tender and lightly browned, about 8 minutes. Reduce the heat to low. Combine the sherry, lemon juice, and paprika in a small bowl. Add to the pan and stir gently until the liquid is nearly evaporated, about 3 minutes. Remove from the heat and stir in the parsley, dash of salt, and dash of pepper. Taste and adjust the seasoning. Cover to keep warm.

Remove and discard the bay leaves. Let the soup cool for a few minutes.

In several batches, purée the soup in a blender until smooth. Return the soup to the pan. Stir in the salt and pepper. Warm, stirring constantly, over medium heat. Taste and adjust the seasoning.

Top each serving with a sprinkling of pepper, a small mound of mushrooms, and a sprig of fennel greens.

Roasted Tomato Soup
with Basil Pesto

I like to make this dish in the summer, using just-picked basil for the pesto, vine-ripened toma-toes for the soup, and Sangiovese to bring out their fresh flavors. The soup is equally delicious served warm or chilled. To make the servings more substantial, garnish with crispy croutons.

MAKES 5 CUPS (*4 servings*) | VEGAN RECIPE

3	pounds (about 10) ripe tomatoes, halved horizontally	4	cloves garlic, minced
4	tablespoons olive oil, divided	¼	cup Sangiovese or other medium-bodied, high-acid red wine
⅛	teaspoon + ¼ teaspoon salt, or to taste	2	tablespoons tomato paste
⅛	teaspoon + ½ teaspoon freshly ground pepper, or to taste	1	teaspoon sugar
1	cup finely chopped onion	1	bay leaf
2	ribs celery, finely chopped		Scant pinch of red-pepper flakes (optional), see Tips
1	fennel bulb, quartered and thinly sliced (see Tips)	⅓	cup Basil Pesto (*page 36*)
			Water or milk, as needed

Preheat the oven to 425°F.

In a large bowl, toss the tomatoes with 2 tablespoons of the oil and ⅛ teaspoon each of the salt and pepper. Arrange the tomatoes, cut side up, on a foil-lined jelly roll pan. Roast the tomatoes in the oven for 10 minutes. Reduce the oven temperature to 300°F and continue roasting for 20 more minutes. Let cool.

Meanwhile, heat the remaining 2 tablespoons of oil in a Dutch oven over medium heat. Add the onion, celery, and fennel and cook, stirring occasionally, until the celery is tender, about 10 minutes. Add the garlic and stir constantly for about 1 minute.

Stir in the tomatoes and the remaining ingredients (including the remaining ¼ teaspoon salt and ½ teaspoon pepper), except the red-pepper flakes, the Basil Pesto, and the water or milk. Cover and cook, stirring occasionally, for 20 minutes. Let cool for a few minutes. Remove the bay leaf.

In several batches, purée the soup in a blender until smooth.

Pass the puréed mixture through a sieve. Return the soup to the pan. Warm, stirring constantly, over medium heat. Add the red-pepper flakes. Taste and adjust the seasoning.

In a small bowl, combine the pesto with a little water or milk until it reaches a cake-batter consistency. Swirl 1 heaping tablespoon of the pesto across the top of each bowl of soup before serving.

TIPS | ❧ *Fresh fennel (also known as anise bulb or finocchio), with its large, white, bulbous base and feathery green leaves, looks like a flattened bunch of celery. Choose firm fennel bulbs with no signs of browning and bright green, fresh-looking tops. Refrigerate, unwashed, in a zip-top plastic bag for up to 6 days.*

To use the bulb, cut it into quarters; remove and discard the core. Cut the quarters into slices or dice. The fibrous stalks are of little use other than for adding to stocks. Snip the foliage as you would dill, to use for delicate flavor or as a garnish. Fennel's distinct licorice flavor becomes milder and sweeter when the vegetable is cooked.

❧ *Red-pepper flakes, also called crushed red pepper, are the seeds and flakes of fiery hot peppers. Use in moderation because a small amount goes a long way. Refrigerate in a tightly covered container to preserve the color and flavor.*

Yukon Gold Potato–Leek Soup

Yukon Gold potatoes, with their warm, buttery hue, and pungent arugula take potato soup beyond its humble reputation. This soup is delicious at any time of the year, but peppery arugula leaves are at their peak in the spring. For a sweeter, more kid-friendly flavor, substitute fresh spinach.

MAKES 6½ CUPS (*6 servings*)

1	tablespoon olive oil	3	sprigs fresh thyme + 6 small sprigs for garnish
1	tablespoon unsalted butter	2	cups milk
2	medium leeks, white parts only, quartered lengthwise and thinly sliced (see Tips, page 61)	1	cup stemmed and torn arugula or 2 cups stemmed and torn salad spinach
1	cup coarsely chopped yellow onion	¼	cup freshly grated Parmesan cheese
2	cloves garlic, minced	¼	cup dry sherry
2	cups vegetable stock (see page 18)	½	teaspoon salt, or to taste
2–3	Yukon gold potatoes (about 24 ounces total), peeled and cut into ½" cubes (about 4 cups)	½	teaspoon freshly ground pepper, or to taste
1	small zucchini, quartered lengthwise and cut into ½" chunks		Sweet paprika (see Tips) and finely shredded sharp Cheddar cheese for garnish

Melt the oil with the butter in a Dutch oven over medium heat. Add the leeks and onion and cook, stirring frequently, until the onions are translucent, about 5 minutes. Add the garlic and stir constantly for about 1 minute.

Stir in the vegetable stock, potatoes, zucchini, and 3 thyme sprigs. Increase the heat to high and bring to a boil. Reduce the heat to low, cover, and simmer until the potatoes are very tender, about 15 minutes. Remove and discard the thyme sprigs. Let the soup cool for a few minutes.

In several batches, purée the soup in a blender until smooth. Return the soup to the pan. Stir in the milk, arugula or spinach, Parmesan, and sherry. Cook over low heat, stirring occasionally, until the arugula or spinach is wilted and the soup is thoroughly heated, about 5 minutes. (Do not let the soup come to a boil.) Stir in the salt and pepper. Taste and adjust the seasoning.

Sprinkle the servings with paprika, top with a small mound of cheese, and garnish with the small thyme sprigs.

TIPS | ❧ *Paprika is made from ground, dried, sweet red peppers. Most paprika comes from Spain, South America, California, or Hungary; the Hungarian variety is considered by many to be the best. Hungarian paprika comes in 3 levels of heat: mild (also called "sweet"), hot, and exceptionally hot. To preserve its color and flavor, store paprika in a cool, dark place for up to 6 months.*

SHERRIED SPLIT PEA SOUP

No ham bones here! This soup gets its special flavor and aroma from the addition of cumin and dry sherry. It always gets raves, even from carnivores.

MAKES 6 CUPS (*6 servings*) | VEGAN RECIPE (*if made with vegetable oil instead of butter and if sour cream garnish is omitted*)

1	tablespoon unsalted butter	1	carrot, cut into ¼" dice
½	cup finely chopped onion (see Tips)	¼	cup dry sherry
		1	bay leaf
1	teaspoon ground cumin	½	teaspoon salt, or to taste
8	cups vegetable stock (see page 18), divided	½	teaspoon freshly ground nutmeg
1½	cups dried split peas (see Tips)		Sour cream for garnish

Melt the butter in a Dutch oven over medium heat. Add the onion and cook, stirring occasionally, until translucent, about 5 minutes. Add the cumin and stir constantly for about 30 seconds.

Stir in 6 cups of the vegetable stock and the split peas. Increase the heat to high and bring to a boil. Reduce the heat and simmer, covered, until the liquid is absorbed, about 45 minutes. Stir occasionally, mashing the peas as you stir.

Add the remaining 2 cups of vegetable stock, the carrot, sherry, bay leaf, salt, and nutmeg. Cover and cook over low heat until the split peas and carrots are tender, about 15 minutes. Taste and adjust the seasoning. Remove the bay leaf before serving.

Garnish the servings with small dollops of sour cream.

TIPS | ❧ *There are 2 basic types of onions: storage and fresh. Storage onions, which are available year-round, are picked at the peak of the summer harvest season and are then "cured" by a drying process that gives them their familiar dry, papery skin. Store them in a cool, dry, well-ventilated spot for up to 2 months; keep them away from potatoes, which give off moisture that causes onions to rot. Among the storage onions, white onions generally have a sharper flavor and stronger bite than yellow onions.*

Early in April, the first fresh onions arrive. These are named after the regions where they're grown—Vidalias from Georgia, Spring Sweets from Texas, Walla Wallas from Washington, Mauis from Hawaii, and OSO Sweets from Chile. These onions are prized for their fruity sweetness and are not the least bit hot. They have thin, shiny skins and are flatter in shape than storage onions. These onions also contain more sugar and water so they do not keep as long; refrigerate them in the vegetable crisper for up to 1 week.

Refrigerating an onion for several hours or freezing it for 20 minutes before chopping can reduce tear-producing vapors. The sulfuric compounds that cause tears are concentrated at the root end of an onion, so it also helps to leave the root end intact while cutting. Fresh onions are lower in the sulfur compounds that give most onions their characteristic bite and their tear-producing properties.

All onions oxidize when cut, so slice or chop onions just before you plan to use them to avoid "off" flavors.

❧ *Field peas are a variety of yellow or green peas grown specifically for drying; in the process, they split along a natural seam and become "dried split peas." They are available in most supermarkets and health food stores. Store in a cool, dry place for up to 1 year. Pick through them before using to discard any discolored or shriveled peas or small pebbles. Because presoaking is not necessary before cooking, they're quick to prepare. Do not add salt to the cooking liquid, because it slows down the cooking time and toughens the peas.*

Roasted Butternut Squash and Pear Bisque

Winter squash are harvested at summer's end, and they remain available throughout the winter. Butternut is a popular, sweet-tasting variety that harbors beta-carotene in its rich orange flesh.

Makes 6 cups (*6 servings*)

1	butternut squash (about 2 pounds), see Tips, page 131
1	tablespoon unsalted butter
2	peeled and coarsely chopped Bartlett pears
1½	cups finely chopped onion
1	tablespoon curry powder
4	cups vegetable stock (see page 18)
½	cup half-and-half
3	tablespoons Cognac or other brandy
¼	teaspoon salt, or to taste
¼	teaspoon freshly ground pepper, or to taste
	Toasted chopped walnuts (see Tips) for garnish

Preheat the oven to 375°F.

Cut the squash in half lengthwise and discard the seeds. Place the squash halves, cut side down, on a foil-lined baking sheet.

Bake for 45 minutes, or until tender. Cool the squash, then remove the pulp (about 2 cups).

Melt the butter in a Dutch oven over medium heat. Add the pear and onion and cook until tender, about 10 minutes. Add the curry powder and stir constantly for about 30 seconds.

Stir in the squash pulp and the vegetable stock. Increase the heat to high and bring to a boil. Reduce the heat to low, then cover and simmer for 20 minutes. Let cool for a few minutes.

In several batches, purée the soup in a blender until smooth.

Return the soup to the pan. Stir in the half-and-half, Cognac, salt, and pepper. Warm, stirring constantly, over medium heat. (Do not let the soup come to a boil.) Taste and adjust the seasoning.

Garnish the servings with walnuts.

TIPS | ❧ *Toasting intensifies the flavor and enhances the texture of most nuts. To toast nuts on the stove top, place them in a single layer in a dry skillet over medium heat. Stir or toss the nuts, watching closely, until they are fragrant and golden brown, about 4 minutes. Or, spread the nuts on a heavy baking sheet or pie plate, and bake in a preheated 350°F oven for about 5 minutes, stirring frequently. To prevent burning, remove the nuts from the skillet or baking pan as soon as they are toasted.*

GINGERED CARROT SOUP

Ginger is a remarkable spice. Traditionally, it lends its sweet heat and unique flavor to Asian and Indian dishes. Here, I've borrowed it to pair with sweet carrots, tart apples, and mellow, aromatic sherry for a light soup that's ideal as a first course.

MAKES 6 CUPS (*6 servings*)

2	tablespoons unsalted butter	1	sprig fresh thyme
1	cup finely chopped yellow onion	1	bay leaf
1	tablespoon minced fresh ginger (see Tips)	3/4	cup half-and-half
		1/4	cup dry sherry
2	cloves garlic, minced	1/4	teaspoon salt, or to taste
4	cups vegetable stock (see page 18)	1/4	teaspoon ground white pepper, or to taste
1 1/2	pounds (about 8) carrots, thinly sliced		
			Finely chopped fresh chives for garnish
1	Granny Smith or other tart apple, peeled and coarsely chopped		

Melt the butter in a Dutch oven over medium heat. Add the onion and cook, stirring occasionally, until translucent, about 5 minutes. Reduce the heat to low and add the ginger and garlic. Stir constantly for about 1 minute.

Stir in the vegetable stock, carrots, apple, thyme, and bay leaf, then increase the heat to high and bring to a boil. Reduce the heat to low, cover, and cook until the carrots are very tender, about 20 minutes. Remove and discard the thyme and bay leaf. Let the soup cool for a few minutes.

In several batches, purée the soup in a blender until smooth.

Return the soup to the pan. Add the half-and-half, sherry, salt, and pepper. Warm, stirring constantly over medium heat. (Do not let the soup come to a boil.) Taste and adjust the seasoning.

Garnish the servings with a sprinkling of chives.

TIPS | ❧ *Fresh, mature ginger should be firm, with a smooth brown skin and no soft spots. To test for freshness, break off 1 of the knobs; if fresh, it will break with a clean snap. Keep ginger at room temperature for up to 1 week, or refrigerate in a plastic bag for up to 2 weeks. Fresh is always best, but for longer storage, tightly wrap whole, unpeeled ginger in aluminum foil or seal it in a zip-top freezer bag for up to 3 months. While the ginger is still frozen, use a fine grater to grate off the amount needed. Rewrap and return the remainder to the freezer. Freezing changes its texture, but the ginger flavor remains.*

Peel fresh or frozen ginger before using and mince it well so the flavor will be distributed evenly in the dish.

Ginger should be used in the form that is specified in the recipe because the flavor varies with each type. For example, ground dried ginger does not have the same distinctive flavor as fresh and should not be substituted for fresh in cooked recipes. It can, however, be used in baked goods.

Fresh Pea Soup with Gremolata

This soup is smoother in texture and fresher and sweeter in flavor—plus it's much quicker to pre-pare—than the traditional version made with dried split peas and flavored with ham. The gre-molata garnish adds contrasting colors, texture, and a fresh minty flavor.

Makes 4½ cups (*4 servings*)

For the soup

2	tablespoons unsalted butter or canola oil	1	cup milk
2	ribs celery, finely chopped	¼	cup sweet vermouth, Gewürztraminer, or other medium-bodied, sweet and fruity white wine
½	cup finely chopped onion		
2	cloves garlic, minced	2	teaspoons sugar
2	cups vegetable stock (see page 18)	¼	teaspoon salt, or to taste
1	bag (16 ounces) frozen baby peas (see Tips)		Dash of ground white pepper, or to taste

For the gremolata

¼	cup crumbled feta cheese	2	tablespoons finely chopped fresh mint
¼	cup diced plum tomato		
2	tablespoons finely chopped fresh flat-leaf parsley	1	teaspoon lemon zest

To make the soup, melt the butter or heat the oil in a Dutch oven over medium heat. Add the celery and onion and cook, stirring occasionally, until the onion is translucent, about 5 minutes. Add the garlic and stir constantly for about 1 minute.

Stir in the vegetable stock and peas. Increase the heat to high and bring to a boil. Reduce the heat, then cover and simmer until the vegetables are very tender, about 5 minutes. Let cool for a few minutes.

In several batches, purée the pea-stock mixture in a blender until smooth.

Return the soup to the pan. Stir in the milk, vermouth, sugar, salt, and white pepper. Warm, stirring constantly, over medium heat. Taste and adjust the seasoning.

To make the gremolata, while the soup is rewarming, stir together all the ingredients in a small bowl.

Top each serving with a heaping tablespoon of the gremolata.

TIPS | ❧ *Generally, the flavor of baby peas, or* petit pois, *is preferable to that of the standard-size peas. Harvested when young, baby peas remain especially sweet after picking; they also retain a brighter color and a firmer texture.*

Roasted Orange–Bell Pepper Soup

This soup has a sunny orange color and a smooth, silky texture that carries a hint of sweetness. It's elegant enough to serve as a first course for company. They'll savor the flavor and vanilla aromas added by the wood-aged Madeira.

Makes 5 cups (*4 servings*)

1	large navel orange	2	tablespoons all-purpose flour
2	yellow bell peppers	¼	cup semisweet Madeira or other fortified, semisweet white wine
2	orange bell peppers		
2	tablespoons unsalted butter	½	teaspoon salt, or to taste
1	cup finely chopped onion	½	teaspoon freshly ground pepper, or to taste (see Tips)
2	carrots, finely grated		
2	cups vegetable stock (see page 18)		Freshly ground pepper, thin peeled orange slices, and finely chopped fresh chives (see Tips) for garnish
1	cup milk		

Position the oven broiler rack about 5" from the heating element. Preheat the broiler. Line a baking sheet with foil.

Slice about ¼" from both ends of the orange, then cut the orange in half crosswise. Place, cut side up, on the prepared baking sheet. Remove the stems from the peppers and cut the peppers in half lengthwise. Discard the seeds, membranes, and stem. Place the pepper halves, skin side up, on the baking sheet and flatten each with the palm of your hand.

Broil the orange and the bell peppers for 8 to 10 minutes, or until the bell peppers are fork-tender and the skins are blackened, charred, and blistered.

Transfer the orange to a plate and let cool. While they are still hot, transfer the peppers to a heavy-duty zip-top plastic bag and seal. Set them aside to cool.

Meanwhile, melt the butter in a medium saucepan over medium heat. Add the onion and carrots and cook, stirring occasionally, until tender, about 6 minutes.

Remove the peppers from the bag. Peel and discard the skins. Coarsely chop the peppers.

Squeeze the juice from the orange.

Process the peppers and orange juice in a blender until smooth. Add the carrot mixture and process again until smooth.

Whisk together the vegetable stock, milk, and flour in a Dutch oven until smooth. Bring to a simmer, stirring constantly, over medium-high heat. Reduce the heat to medium and stir in the bell pepper mixture, Madeira, salt, and pepper. Simmer, stirring occasionally, for about 10 minutes. Taste and adjust the seasoning.

Garnish the servings with pepper, orange slices, and chives.

TIPS | ❧ *Peppercorns are berries that grow in grapelike clusters on a climbing vine. Black peppercorns are picked when the berries are not quite ripe, then dried in the sun until they wrinkle and turn from dark brown to black. To produce white peppercorns, the berries are allowed to ripen longer. When they turn a yellowish red, they are soaked in water to remove the outer skin and are then dried. White pepper is milder, and for appearance's sake is often recommended for light-colored soups and sauces.*

Peppercorns can be stored in a cool, dark place for about 1 year. Ground pepper keeps about 3 months. For full flavor, it's always best to grind pepper just before using.

❧ *Chives are members of the onion family. Potted chives are freshest; use scissors to snip off whole blades rather than chopping the tops off all the blades. If you buy cut chives, wrap them in a damp paper towel, seal in a plastic bag, and refrigerate for up to 1 week. Add chives to a dish toward the end of the cooking time to help retain flavor. Do not substitute dried chives for fresh; use the green part of scallions cut into thin strips instead.*

CHILLED PROSECCO-MELON SOUP

This elegant chilled soup is a favorite of my friend and creative cook, Fran Lebahn. Following her lead, I find it's perfect to begin brunch on a sunny summer morning. It's bright, pretty, and refreshing. And nothing draws oohs and ahs like something bubbly.

The soup can be prepared in advance, but to retain effervescence, add the sparkling spirit just before serving. As you savor its brilliance, remember Dom Pérignon's comment at the moment of his discovery of Champagne: "Come quickly, I am tasting the stars!"

MAKES 5 CUPS (*4 to 6 servings*) | VEGAN RECIPE (*if whipped cream is omitted*)

2	cups coarsely chopped cantaloupe	¾	cup Prosecco, sparkling Moscato, or other semisweet sparkling white wine
2	cups coarsely chopped honeydew melon		
1	cup fresh orange juice (see Tips)		Sweetened whipped cream and lime zest for garnish
1	tablespoon fresh lime juice		
1	tablespoon honey, or to taste		

Purée the cantaloupe, honeydew, orange juice, lime juice, and honey in a blender until smooth. Refrigerate in a covered container until chilled, at least 3 hours, before serving.

Just before serving, stir in the wine. Taste and adjust the sweetening.

Top each serving with a dollop of whipped cream and sprinkle with lime zest.

TIPS | ❧ *When selecting citrus fruits for juicing, choose those that have a fine-textured skin and are heavy for their size. To squeeze more juice from citrus fruits, first bring them to room temperature, or microwave chilled fruit (piercing the fruit with a fork or knife first) for 30 seconds on high. Then roll the fruit around on a hard surface, pressing hard with the palm of your hand to break the inner membranes.*

SWEET STRAWBERRY-MADEIRA SOUP

For a festive presentation, swirl Raspberry-Merlot Sauce (page 213) or Hot Fudge Sauce (page 212) across the surface of this chilled soup. Sometimes, I use it as the first course to launch a meal, but it's equally delightful as a dessert.

MAKES 2 CUPS (*4 servings*)

2	cups sliced fresh strawberries	1	tablespoon sugar, or to taste
1	cup plain yogurt (see Tips)		Sprigs of fresh mint for garnish
¼	cup semisweet Madeira or other fortified, semisweet white wine		

Purée all the soup ingredients, except the garnish, in a blender until smooth. Taste and adjust the sweetening.

Refrigerate in a covered container until chilled, at least 3 hours, before serving.

Garnish the servings with mint sprigs.

TIPS | ❧ *It's best to use yogurt when it is fresh, but it will keep for up to 10 days after the sell-by date on the container.*

SALADS

Among wine enthusiasts, debate rages as to the compatibility of wines and salads, so it seems that wines are rarely used in the preparation of salads. In the process of developing these recipes, I found that the keys to success lie in heating some wines long enough to soften their flavors, as well as in the use of sweet, fruity wines, which require no alteration to work well in salads.

Basil-Sherry Vinaigrette (*page 91*), made with sweet sherry, is heated with the beans just before serving on the

Warm Butter Bean Salad *(page 88)*. The red wine in Sangiovese Vinaigrette *(page 93)* is simmered and reduced, which evaporates much of the alcohol. The wine is then combined with extra-virgin olive oil to balance the acidity.

The natural sugars in Gewürztraminer and Muscat create harmony and balance the other salad ingredients. Tequila and Merlot are used uncooked in fruit salads. And Pears Poached in Crème de Cassis *(page 87)* are delicious by themselves, but they make an especially lovely presentation as part of Poached Pear Salad with Walnut Vinaigrette *(page 86)*.

Note that the dressings in this chapter are seasoned to taste with salt and pepper. When tasted from a spoon, most dressings will seem very strong, so it's best to taste by dipping a salad ingredient, such as a leaf of lettuce, into the dressing.

These *spirited vegetarian* salads can be served alone as a light lunch, as an accompaniment to soups, or as an innovative course in your dinner menu. ❧

Wheat Berry–Bean Salad

For a lunch that's both light and satisfying, accompany this healthful salad with a creamy soup, such as Fresh Pea Soup with Gremolata (page 76) or Roasted Tomato Soup with Basil Pesto (page 66), and crispy crackers.

Makes 6 servings | Vegan recipe

4	cups water	1	can (15 ounces) chickpeas, drained and rinsed
1	cup wheat berries	¼	cup fresh lemon juice
2	tablespoons olive oil	2	tablespoons coarsely chopped fresh flat-leaf parsley
1	cup coarsely chopped red onion	¼	teaspoon salt, or to taste
2	cups sliced cremini mushrooms (about 6 ounces)	¼	teaspoon freshly ground pepper, or to taste
½	cup Gewürztraminer or other medium-bodied, sweet and fruity white wine		Sprigs of flat-leaf parsley

Bring the water to a boil in a large saucepan over high heat. Add a dash of salt. Rinse the wheat berries in a strainer under cool water, then add to the saucepan. When the water returns to a boil, reduce the heat to low. Cover and simmer, adding more water if necessary, until the wheat berries are tender, about 1 hour. Drain if necessary. Spread the wheat berries on a baking sheet to cool.

Meanwhile, heat the oil in a medium sauté pan over medium heat. Add the onion and cook, stirring occasionally, until translucent, about 5 minutes. Stir in the mushrooms and wine, then simmer, uncovered, stirring occasionally, until the mushrooms are tender, about 8 minutes.

Transfer the wheat berries to a medium bowl. Stir in the mushroom mixture and the remaining ingredients, except the garnish. Taste and adjust the seasoning.

Transfer the salad to a covered container and refrigerate for at least 2 hours or for up to 3 days. Serve chilled or at room temperature. Garnish with parsley sprigs.

POACHED PEAR SALAD
WITH WALNUT VINAIGRETTE

Here's a salad that's worthy of praise from your most discriminating guests. The components require advance planning, but the plates can be assembled quickly and with artistry just before serving. If you're tempted to gild the lily—or pear—drizzle the edge of the plates with Raspberry-Merlot Sauce (page 213).

MAKES 4 SERVINGS

1	tablespoon unsalted butter	$1/2$	teaspoon packed brown sugar
1	tablespoon light corn syrup	$1/8$	teaspoon salt, or to taste
1	teaspoon water	$1/8$	teaspoon freshly ground pepper, or to taste
$1/4$	teaspoon salt		
1	cup walnut halves	4	cups stemmed baby spinach leaves
2	tablespoons walnut oil, preferably roasted walnut oil (see Tips)	2	Pears Poached in Crème de Cassis (*opposite page*), at room temperature, cut into $1/2$" slices
2	tablespoons red wine vinegar	$1/3$	cup crumbled blue cheese
$1/2$	teaspoon Dijon mustard		

Preheat the oven to 250°F. Line a jelly roll pan with foil and lightly coat with cooking spray. Melt the butter in a small saucepan over medium heat. Stir in the corn syrup, water, and salt, and bring to a boil. Add the walnuts and stir until coated. Spread the nuts in a single layer on the prepared pan. Bake, stirring occasionally, for 60 minutes. Use a spatula to transfer the nuts to a plate. (They'll become crisper as they cool.)

Whisk together the oil, vinegar, mustard, brown sugar, salt, and pepper in a small bowl. Taste and adjust the seasoning.

Toss the spinach with about three-fourths of the vinaigrette in a medium bowl. Divide the spinach between 4 salad plates. Arrange the pear slices over the spinach and drizzle with the remaining vinaigrette. Sprinkle with the cheese and walnuts.

Walnut oil has a distinctive, nutty taste and is used mainly for salads rather than as a cooking medium. You'll find it in many supermarkets and gourmet food stores. For the best flavor, buy roasted walnut oil. Because it turns rancid quickly, refrigerate after opening; it will keep for up to 3 months.

Pears Poached in Crème de Cassis

These pears also make a luxurious dessert. If you'd prefer, poach the pears whole, which will require a few more minutes, and serve them at room temperature drizzled with the syrup.

Makes 4 servings | Vegan recipe

1	cup crème de cassis	¼	cup sugar
1	cup Shiraz or other full-bodied, ripe-jammy red wine	1	cinnamon stick
	Zest of 1 lemon	4	pears, cored, peeled, and halved
2	tablespoons fresh lemon juice		

Combine the crème de cassis, wine, lemon zest, lemon juice, sugar, and cinnamon stick in a large (preferably nonstick) saucepan. Bring to a boil over medium heat. Reduce the heat to medium-low and simmer, uncovered, for 10 minutes.

Add the pears, cover, and simmer until a paring knife easily pierces the pears, about 10 minutes. Using a slotted spoon, transfer the pears to a plate and let cool.

Reduce the heat to low. Remove and discard the cinnamon stick. Continue to cook the sauce, uncovered, until it is reduced to maple-syrup consistency, about 20 minutes. Watch closely. (The sauce thickens as it cools.)

Serve the room-temperature pears drizzled with the sauce.

Warm Butter Bean Salad with Basil-Sherry Vinaigrette

Served warm, this robust winter salad is hearty enough to stand on its own. The sweet bell pepper and salty feta cheese complement the peppery arugula leaves. To complete the meal, pass a loaf of crusty artisan bread.

MAKES 4 SERVINGS | VEGAN RECIPE (*if feta cheese garnish is omitted*)

8	leaves romaine lettuce, coarsely shredded	2	cloves garlic, minced
16	leaves arugula (see Tips)	1	can (15 ounces) butter beans, drained and rinsed
1	tablespoon olive oil	½	cup Basil-Sherry Vinaigrette (*page 91*)
2	carrots, coarsely shredded		
½	red bell pepper, coarsely chopped		Freshly ground pepper and crumbled feta cheese (see Tips) for garnish
¼	cup coarsely chopped red onion		

Spread a layer of lettuce on 4 large salad plates. Arrange the arugula leaves atop the lettuce, radiating from the center, sunburst fashion.

Heat the oil in a medium nonstick skillet over medium heat. Add the carrots, bell pepper, and onion. Cook, stirring occasionally, until the bell pepper is crisp-tender, about 5 minutes. Add the garlic and stir constantly for about 1 minute. Reduce the heat to low. Add the beans and the vinaigrette and gently stir until warm, about 4 minutes.

Spoon the bean mixture over the arugula. Serve warm, garnished with pepper and feta cheese.

TIPS | ❧ *Arugula, also called roquette or "rocket," is a long, spear-shaped leaf with a spicy, peppery, mustardlike bitterness and aroma. Select dark green leaves no more than 5" long; the more mature the green, the stronger the flavor. Wrap the roots in moist paper towels and place them in a plastic bag, then store in the refrigerator for up to 2 days. Wash the sandy leaves thoroughly before using.*

❧ *Feta cheese is a white Greek cheese with a rich, tangy flavor. Traditionally, it is made with goat's milk, sheep's milk, or a combination; today it is also often made with cow's milk. In some markets, you will find varieties flavored with peppercorns or herbs. Feta is crumbly when fresh, drier and saltier when mature.*

Orzo Salad
with Basil-Sherry Vinaigrette

Orzo, riso, and rosamarina are tiny, rice-shaped pastas stocked with the Italian foods in most supermarkets or Italian specialty stores. Instead of frozen corn, when it's available, I like to substitute fresh corn cut from the cob after roasting or boiling. Do as the Italians do and include this dish among an assortment of antipasti, or give it star billing as a light lunch.

MAKES 4 SERVINGS | VEGAN RECIPE

¾ cup orzo, riso, or rosamarina pasta

1 cup frozen white shoepeg corn kernels, thawed (see Tips)

2 plum tomatoes, cut into ½" cubes

½ cup Basil-Sherry Vinaigrette (*opposite page*)

Salt and freshly ground pepper to taste

4 leaves butter lettuce or other soft-leafed lettuce

Small sprigs of fresh basil for garnish

Bring a small saucepan of salted water to a boil. Cook the pasta according to the package directions. Drain well. Rinse with cool water and drain again.

In a medium bowl, toss together the pasta, corn, and tomatoes. Add ¼ cup of the vinaigrette and toss again.

Refrigerate the salad and the remaining vinaigrette in separate covered containers for at least 2 hours or for up to 2 days. Serve the salad chilled or at room temperature. Toss with the remaining vinaigrette just before serving. Taste and add salt and pepper as desired.

Spoon the salad onto lettuce-lined salad plates and garnish with basil sprigs.

TIPS | ❦ *White shoepeg corn kernels, named for their peglike shape, are available frozen. The kernels are smaller and sweeter than regular yellow corn kernels.*

Basil-Sherry Vinaigrette

This vinaigrette brings out the best in garden-fresh tomatoes. It's also lovely tossed with an orzo, corn, and tomato salad (opposite page) or heated with a warm bean salad (page 88). The key to top-notch flavor: Use extra-virgin olive oil and fresh basil.

Makes ½ cup | Vegan recipe

¼	cup extra-virgin olive oil	2	tablespoons minced shallot (see Tips)
3	tablespoons sweet (cream) sherry	¼	teaspoon salt, or to taste
1	tablespoon fresh lemon juice	¼	teaspoon freshly ground pepper, or to taste
¼	cup finely chopped fresh basil or 1 teaspoon dried basil		

Whisk together the oil, sherry, and lemon juice in a small bowl. Stir in the remaining ingredients. Taste and adjust the seasoning.

Refrigerate in a covered container for up to 4 days. Whisk or shake before serving.

TIPS | ❧ *Shallots, a member of the onion family, are small, bulbous herbs with a mild onion-garlic flavor. Always use fresh—never dried—shallots; if fresh are unavailable, substitute some onion and garlic. Store shallots in a cool, dark place for up to 1 month; use before they begin to sprout. When sautéing, don't allow shallots to brown or they will taste bitter.*

ITALIAN BREAD SALAD
WITH SANGIOVESE VINAIGRETTE

This comforting salad, traditionally called panzanella, *was developed by frugal Italian women as a practical and tasty use for day-old bread. For authentic flavor, use top-quality, juicy, vine-ripened tomatoes and rustic bread. As the toasted bread cubes soak up some of the aromatic red wine vinaigrette, they soften to an appealing, chewy texture. The salad is substantial enough to make a light meal on its own, or serve it as the first course for an Italian feast.*

MAKES 6 SERVINGS | VEGAN RECIPE

3	cups thick-crusted Italian or French bread in ¾" cubes	2	tablespoons capers, drained and rinsed
1	pound (about 3) beefsteak tomatoes, cut into ½" cubes	¾	cup Sangiovese Vinaigrette (*opposite page*)
1	medium cucumber, peeled, halved lengthwise, seeded, and cut into ¼" slices	6	large leaves butterhead or Boston lettuce
¼	cup finely chopped red onion		Freshly ground pepper for garnish
¼	cup coarsely chopped fresh basil leaves		

Preheat the oven to 350°F.

Spread the bread cubes in a single layer on a baking sheet and toast in the preheated oven for about 8 to 10 minutes, or until lightly browned and crisp. Set aside to cool.

Toss together the remaining salad ingredients, except the vinaigrette, lettuce leaves, and garnish, in a large bowl. Add the vinaigrette and toss again. Taste and adjust the seasoning. Five minutes before serving, toss in the bread cubes.

Mound the salad atop 1 lettuce leaf on each plate, and garnish with pepper.

SANGIOVESE VINAIGRETTE

Reducing wine concentrates the flavor in this lovely ruby-colored dressing.

MAKES ⅔ CUP | VEGAN RECIPE

¾	cup Sangiovese or other medium-bodied, high-acid red wine	1	teaspoon packed brown sugar, or to taste
1	tablespoon balsamic vinegar (see Tips)	½	teaspoon mustard powder
1	clove garlic, minced	¼	teaspoon salt, or to taste
¼	cup extra-virgin olive oil	¼	teaspoon freshly ground pepper, or to taste
2	tablespoons coarsely chopped fresh flat-leaf parsley		

Bring the wine to a boil in a small saucepan over high heat. Reduce the heat to medium-low and simmer, uncovered, until the wine is reduced by half, about 8 minutes. Stir in the vinegar and garlic. Continue to simmer until the garlic has softened, about 1 more minute. Transfer the mixture to a bowl and cool to room temperature. Whisk in the remaining ingredients. Taste and adjust the seasoning. Refrigerate in a covered container for up to 1 week. Whisk before using.

TIPS | *Balsamic vinegar is made by boiling the juice of white Trebbiano grapes in copper pots until it caramelizes. True balsamic is then aged for up to 100 years, in barrels made from various woods (oak, chestnut, mulberry, and juniper). The result has a heavy, mellow, almost-sweet flavor, and a dark color. Inexpensive imitations that lack the distinctive flavor complexity are made from red wine vinegar that has been fortified with concentrated grape juice and caramelized sugar.*

Fresh Mozzarella Salad with Sangiovese Vinaigrette

For me, the flavor of a juicy, ripe tomato amply kissed by the sun is the essence of summer. If you don't grow your own, you'll find homegrown quality at farm stands and farmers' markets. I've personalized this traditional Italian salad with Sangiovese Vinaigrette. Serve it as a light lunch with a basket of crusty bread or as a delicious prelude to an Italian entrée.

MAKES 4 SERVINGS

8	ounces fresh mozzarella cheese, cut into 12 thin slices (see Tips)
2	beefsteak tomatoes, each cut into 6 slices (see Tips)
12	large basil leaves

¼ cup Sangiovese Vinaigrette (*page 93*)

Freshly ground pepper for garnish

On each of 4 salad plates, arrange the cheese slices, tomato slices, and basil leaves alternately in an overlapping row. Drizzle each salad with about 1 tablespoon of the vinaigrette and sprinkle with pepper.

TIPS | ❦ *Fresh mozzarella cheese—a far cry from packaged "pizza cheese"—is a mild and sweet-tasting, white, fresh Italian cheese traditionally made only from the milk of water buffaloes. Today, however, most is made with cow's milk. It is usually packaged in whey or water and is often labeled "Italian style." You can find fresh mozzarella in some supermarkets, or in cheese shops or Italian markets.*

❦ *It's best to buy locally grown, vine-ripened tomatoes. But, if it's necessary to ripen tomatoes, put them with an apple in a paper bag pierced with a few holes and let stand at room temperature for 2 to 3 days. Once ripened, do not refrigerate; temperatures below 55°F make tomatoes spongy and destroy their flavor.*

Rice Salad
with Herbed Muscat Dressing

Here's a perfect destination for leftover cooked rice. To keep the nuts crunchy, add them after chilling and just before serving the salad.

MAKES 6 SERVINGS | VEGAN RECIPE

¼	cup Muscat or other sweet, dessert-style white wine
½	cup golden raisins
2	tablespoons olive oil
2	tablespoons fresh lemon juice
1	tablespoon finely chopped fresh tarragon or ½ teaspoon dried tarragon
2	teaspoons Dijon mustard
2	cloves garlic, minced
¼	teaspoon salt, or to taste

¼	teaspoon freshly ground pepper, or to taste
2	cups cooked long-grain white, brown, or basmati rice, at room temperature
¼	cup ripe olives, pitted and quartered
½	cup toasted pine nuts (see Tips, page 73)
1	scallion, both white and green parts, finely chopped

Heat the wine in a small saucepan over medium heat until just warm, then add the raisins. Let stand until the raisins are plump, about 15 minutes, or longer if the raisins are dry.

Whisk together the oil, lemon juice, tarragon, mustard, garlic, salt, and pepper in a small bowl. Stir in the raisins and wine.

Toss the rice with the olives, pine nuts, and scallions in a medium bowl. Add the dressing and toss again. Taste and adjust the seasoning.

Asian Noodle Salad with Peanut Dressing

While Italian pastas are defined by their shape, Asian noodles are named according to their primary ingredient: rice, beans, or wheat, which is used in this recipe.

MAKES 4 SERVINGS | VEGAN RECIPE

For the dressing

¼ cup Riesling or other medium-bodied, high-acid, semisweet white wine

¼ cup smooth peanut butter

3 tablespoons soy sauce

2 tablespoons toasted (Asian) sesame oil

1 tablespoon minced fresh ginger

1 tablespoon sugar

2 cloves garlic, minced

⅛ teaspoon red-pepper flakes

For the salad

6 ounces thin Asian wheat-flour noodles

12 snow peas, strings removed, blanched, halved lengthwise

½ cup sliced white mushrooms

½ red bell pepper, cut into 2" × ¼" strips

2 scallions, both white and green parts, thinly sliced

1 carrot, coarsely shredded

Mandarin orange segments and black sesame seeds

Whisk together all the dressing ingredients in a small bowl.

Cook the noodles according to package directions. Drain well and transfer to a large bowl. Add the dressing to the hot noodles and toss. Let stand until cool. Toss in the remaining ingredients, except the garnish. Serve at room temperature or chilled. Garnish the servings with orange segments and sprinkle with sesame seeds.

Sesame Noodle Salad

Udon are wheat-flour noodles that can be round or flat and range from wide and thick to thin and delicate. For this dish, I usually choose ⅛"-wide, flat udon noodles.

Makes 6 servings | Vegan recipe

8	ounces udon noodles
¼	cup soy sauce
¼	cup mirin (Japanese rice wine)
3	tablespoons toasted (Asian) sesame oil
2	tablespoons toasted sesame seeds (see Tips, page 133)
2	tablespoons coarsely chopped fresh cilantro
1	tablespoon white rice vinegar
⅛	teaspoon red-pepper flakes, or to taste

	Dash of ground white pepper, or to taste
12	asparagus spears, cut into 2" lengths
1	carrot, coarsely shredded
½	cup finely chopped red bell pepper
2	scallions, both white and green parts, finely chopped
	Black sesame seeds and sprigs of fresh cilantro for garnish

Cook the noodles according to package directions.

While the noodles are cooking, whisk together the soy sauce, mirin, sesame oil, sesame seeds, cilantro, vinegar, red-pepper flakes, and white pepper in a small bowl.

Steam the asparagus until crisp-tender, about 5 minutes, and drain well.

Rinse the noodles with cool water. Drain and transfer to a large bowl. Add the sauce and toss, then add the asparagus and the remaining ingredients, except the garnish. Transfer the noodles to a covered container and refrigerate until chilled. Before serving, taste and adjust the seasoning. Garnish with sesame seeds and cilantro.

Potato Salad
with Red Zinfandel Dressing

Enjoy this delicious potato salad either warm or chilled. If refrigerated, serve it later the same day because it will become dry as the dressing soaks into the potatoes.

Makes 4 servings

1	pound (about 6) small red potatoes, scrubbed and halved	½	cup Red Zinfandel Dressing (*opposite page*)
2	tablespoons chopped onion	¼	cup finely chopped fresh flat-leaf parsley
½	teaspoon salt		Dash of salt, or to taste
½	teaspoon freshly ground pepper		Dash of freshly ground pepper, or to taste
2	plum tomatoes, cut into ½" cubes		Sprigs of fresh flat-leaf parsley for garnish
½	red bell pepper, finely chopped		
2	scallions, both white and green parts, finely chopped		
2	tablespoons capers, drained and rinsed		

Bring a large pot of water to a boil over high heat. Add the potatoes, onion, salt, and pepper. Reduce the heat and simmer until the potatoes are just tender, about 12 minutes. Drain well. Halve the potato sections or cut into large chunks.

In a large bowl, toss the potatoes with the tomatoes, bell pepper, scallions, and capers. Add the dressing and parsley, then toss again. Add the salt and pepper. Taste and adjust the seasoning.

Serve warm or refrigerate in a covered container until chilled. Garnish the servings with parsley sprigs.

Red Zinfandel Dressing

This dressing brings a warm potato salad (opposite page) to life but also turns a juicy sliced tomato on lettuce into a work of art.

Makes ½ cup

¼	cup mayonnaise	2	cloves garlic, minced (see Tips)
2	tablespoons Red Zinfandel, Shiraz, or other full-bodied, ripe-jammy red wine	½	teaspoon freshly ground pepper, or to taste
1	tablespoon red wine vinegar	¼	teaspoon salt, or to taste

Whisk together all the ingredients in a small bowl. Taste and adjust the seasoning. Refrigerate in a covered container for up to 3 days.

TIPS | ❧ *Select garlic bulbs that are clean and firm to the touch. Store the whole bulbs in a cool, dark, well-ventilated place, away from heat and direct sunlight. You can purchase a covered clay garlic jar with holes in the side, designed to create these conditions. Or, you can use a small, uncovered dish placed in a kitchen cupboard. When sealed in plastic, garlic may become moldy, and when stored in the refrigerator, the flavor diminishes. If the garlic is plump and fresh, it should keep for up to 8 weeks. Discard it when it loses moisture, shrivels, or sends out green shoots.*

To peel garlic, place the flat blade of a chef's knife over a garlic clove, then pound assertively with the heel of your hand to flatten the clove. This cracks the peel, making it easy to remove, and automatically crushes the garlic.

Garlic develops a bitter taste if allowed to brown, so cook it for 1 minute or less or add it when there is an abundance of moisture in the pan.

RASPBERRY VINEGAR

A bottle of this ruby-colored vinegar, made with her husband's garden-fresh raspberries, was an inspiring gift from my friend Fran Lebahn. While most recipes call for white wine vinegar, Fran's version also incorporates wine. This recipe is simple to multiply, making it an easy-to-prepare and welcome gift from your kitchen, as well as a must in your own. Frozen berries, surprisingly, work just as well as fresh. You can substitute red wine, such as Zinfandel or Shiraz; the color will be redder but the flavor less sweet. (If you'd like, add 1 or 2 tablespoons more sugar.)

MAKES 2 CUPS | VEGAN RECIPE

3	cups (about 20 ounces) frozen unsweetened raspberries, thawed, or fresh red raspberries (see Tips, opposite page)
1	cup white wine vinegar

⅔	cup Gewürztraminer, or other medium-bodied, sweet and fruity white wine
¼	cup sugar

Pour the berries into a glass bowl and crush using a potato masher. Stir in the vinegar and wine. Cover and let stand in a cool place for at least 24 to 48 hours.

Pour the mixture through a fine mesh sieve lined with cheesecloth into a medium nonaluminum saucepan, pressing to extract as much fruit pulp and juice as possible. Add the sugar, then stir constantly over medium heat until the sugar is dissolved, about 3 minutes. Remove from the heat and let cool to room temperature.

Strain the mixture again through a paper coffee filter. (This second straining is not absolutely necessary but will yield a more transparent vinegar.)

Pour the vinegar into clean glass bottles and cap tightly. The vinegar will keep in the refrigerator for up to 3 months.

RASPBERRY-WALNUT VINAIGRETTE

This is one of my favorite vinaigrettes. There are so many ways to use it: Drizzle it over roasted and sliced red beets and garnish with crumbled feta cheese; pour it over sliced fresh pears arranged on a bed of romaine lettuce and garnish with toasted chopped walnuts; or use it to make a simple green salad sing. For a sweeter vinaigrette, add ¹⁄₂ teaspoon or more packed brown sugar.

MAKES ¹⁄₂ CUP | VEGAN RECIPE

¹⁄₄	cup Raspberry Vinegar (*opposite page*)	¹⁄₂	teaspoon packed brown sugar
¹⁄₄	cup walnut oil	¹⁄₄	teaspoon salt, or to taste
1	tablespoon fresh lemon juice	¹⁄₄	teaspoon freshly ground pepper, or to taste
¹⁄₂	teaspoon Dijon mustard		
1	tablespoon finely chopped fresh flat-leaf parsley		

Whisk together all the ingredients in a small bowl. Taste and adjust the seasoning.

Refrigerate in a tightly closed container for up to 3 days. Whisk or shake before serving.

TIPS | ❧ *Because raspberries don't travel well, it's best to buy locally grown varieties. Select brightly colored, plump raspberries with no sign of mold and without hulls. If still attached, the hulls show that the berries were picked too early and may be tart. If the container liner is soaked with juice, the berries may have been sitting for a long time and begun to soften.*

At home, refrigerate raspberries at once, either in the original carton or spread out in a single layer on a dish lined with a paper towel. Plan to use within a day or so. Rinse lightly with cool water and pat dry with paper towels just before serving.

APPLE-RASPBERRY VINAIGRETTE

This sweet vinaigrette is great with fruit. My son, who is not a fan of salads, has 2 generous help-ings when I toss Apple-Raspberry Vinaigrette with romaine lettuce, fresh strawberries, grapes, and toasted sliced almonds. For a simple but luscious salad, you can also drizzle it over a fan of sliced avocado.

MAKES ½ CUP | VEGAN RECIPE

¼ cup frozen apple juice concentrate, thawed (not diluted)

3 tablespoons Raspberry Vinegar (*page 100*)

2 tablespoons canola oil

1 tablespoon honey

¼ teaspoon poppy seeds (see Tips)

⅛ teaspoon mustard powder

⅛ teaspoon salt, or to taste

Whisk together all the ingredients in a small bowl. Taste and adjust the seasoning.

Refrigerate in a tightly closed container for up to 1 week. Whisk or shake before serving.

TIPS | ❧ *Poppy seeds provide a crunchy texture and a nutty flavor. Because of their high oil content, they are prone to rancidity; store them in an airtight container for up to 6 months in the refrigerator.*

CURRIED CARROT-APPLE SALAD

When I yearn for the sensuous flavors of India, I stir up this aromatic salad. It's best to make this dish ahead because the flavors develop as they stand, and the sweet and hot qualities blend nicely.

MAKES 6 SERVINGS

2	tablespoons unsalted butter	2	cups cooked basmati rice, at room temperature (see Tips)
3	carrots, thinly sliced		
2	McIntosh (or other slightly tart) apples, peeled and coarsely chopped	½	cup golden raisins
		¼	teaspoon salt, or to taste
1	tablespoon curry powder	¼	cup toasted slivered almonds (see Tips, page 73)
1	teaspoon celery seeds		
¼	cup Gewürztraminer or other medium-bodied, sweet and fruity white wine		

Melt the butter in a large skillet over medium heat. Add the carrots and cook, stirring occasionally, until crisp-tender, about 5 minutes. Add the apples and continue to cook, stirring occasionally, until the carrots and apples are tender, about 5 more minutes. Add the curry powder and celery seeds, then stir for about 30 seconds. Add the wine, rice, raisins, and salt. Stir gently until evenly combined. Taste and adjust the seasoning.

Refrigerate in a covered container for at least 3 hours. Add the almonds just before serving. Serve chilled or at room temperature.

TIPS | *Basmati, the most famous aromatic rice, is grown in the foothills of the Himalaya Mountains, where it is aged for 2 to 3 years before being milled and sold. Both white and brown varieties have a nutty, buttery flavor. In cooking, the long rice grains remain flaky and separate. Like other rices, 1 cup uncooked basmati rice makes about 3 cups cooked.*

Honeydew Melon Salad

Make the Raspberry-Merlot Sauce in advance. In my opinion, it's an essential element, not only for the color it brings to the plate but also for the surprising flavor component it adds to wake up the salad.

MAKES 4 SERVINGS | VEGAN RECIPE

1	teaspoon honey	1	tablespoon extra-virgin olive oil
1	teaspoon + 1 tablespoon fresh lime juice	2	cups stemmed arugula leaves or fresh baby spinach
2	pinches of salt, divided		Dash of freshly ground pepper
	Four 1½"-thick honeydew melon wedges, peeled (see Tips)	¾	cup Raspberry-Merlot Sauce (*page 213*)

Position the oven broiler rack about 5" from the heating element. Preheat the broiler.

In a small bowl, whisk together the honey, 1 teaspoon of the lime juice, and a pinch of salt. Place the melon wedges, concave side up, on a foil-lined jelly roll pan. Use a basting brush to coat the tops of the melon wedges with the honey mixture.

Stir together the remaining 1 tablespoon lime juice, the olive oil, and the remaining pinch of salt in a medium bowl. Add the arugula and toss. Spread a layer on each of 4 salad plates.

Broil the melon wedges for 3 minutes, or until warm.

To serve, arrange the warm melon wedges atop the arugula, then sprinkle lightly with pepper. Drizzle about 3 tablespoons of the raspberry sauce around the arugula on each plate. Serve immediately while warm.

TIPS | ❧ *The best melons are available in the summer, when the conditions are ideal for these fruits to ripen. Choose a heavy melon with no soft spots, and look for a greenish-yellow rather than a greenish-white skin. Slightly underripe melons can stand at room temperature for a few days to further develop flavor, aroma, and texture. Whole ripe melons will last for about a week in the refrigerator and plastic-wrapped cut ones for about 2 to 3 days. If the seeds rattle when the melon is shaken, it is probably overripe.*

It's best to halve a melon and cut it into wedges, then remove the rind. So, before slicing a melon, always scrub the rind with a soft brush and rinse well. Health safety experts warn that cutting through the rind can transfer bacteria from the rind to the edible part.

SANGRIA FRUIT SALAD

I fell in love with sangria as a favorite refreshment when I visited Spain. Generally, it's a drink that goes unnoticed in serious wine circles because the wine is diluted with fruit juice, liqueur, and sugar, but too bad for wine snobs! In my opinion, it's a fun way to enjoy your daily fruit requirement. In this version, the usual proportions of wine to fruit are altered, transforming the drink into a summer salad or dessert in the Spanish style.

MAKES 6 SERVINGS | VEGAN RECIPE

1	cup Merlot or other full-bodied, plummy red wine	1	peach, peeled and cut into ½" cubes
¼	cup Cognac or brandy	1	pear, peeled and cut into ½" cubes
¼	cup fresh orange juice	1	apple, peeled and cut into ½" cubes
2	tablespoons sugar		
1	orange, scrubbed	1	cup dark seedless grapes, halved
12	whole cloves (see Tips)		Thin orange and lemon slices and sprigs of fresh mint for garnish
½	lemon, scrubbed and coarsely chopped		

Combine the wine, Cognac, orange juice, and sugar in a large bowl. Whisk until the sugar is dissolved.

Peel the orange. Cut the peel into 1" strips and stud them with the cloves. Cut the orange flesh into ½" cubes. Add the peel and cubes to the wine mixture. Stir in the remaining ingredients, except the garnish. Cover and let the mixture stand at room temperature for about 2 hours.

Remove and discard the lemon chunks and clove-studded orange peel, then refrigerate the fruit-wine mixture.

Serve the chilled fruit in long-stemmed wine glasses. Spoon some of the wine mixture over each serving, adorn the edges of the glasses with orange or lemon slices, and garnish with mint sprigs.

TIPS | ❦ *Cloves, which are reddish-brown and tack-shaped, are the dried, unopened flower bud of the tropical evergreen clove tree. They are sold both whole and ground. As with other spices, store cloves in an airtight container in a cool, dark place for no more than 1 year. It's a good idea to date the container before storing.*

Tropical Fruit Salad

Here's a taste of the tropics fit for a scorching day. The sweet tequila sauce is also delicious on cantaloupe and honeydew melon. Feel free to improvise with other fruits (up to 4 cups total).

Makes 4 servings | Vegan recipe

For the sauce

2	tablespoons fresh lime juice	1	tablespoon tequila
2	tablespoons sugar	½	teaspoon lime zest

For the salad

1	cup pineapple in 1" chunks	1	papaya, cut into 1" chunks
1	mango, cut into 1" chunks (see Tips)	1	kiwifruit, cut into ½" chunks

To make the sauce, combine the lime juice and sugar in a small bowl and stir until the sugar is dissolved. Stir in the remaining sauce ingredients.

To complete the salad, combine all the fruit in a medium bowl. Add the sauce and toss. Refrigerate in a covered container for at least 2 or up to 8 hours. Serve cold.

TIPS | ❧ *Mangoes are usually sold quite firm. Ripen them, uncovered, at room temperature, turning occasionally. As the fruit ripens, the skin will change from green to yellow with red mottling, the fruit will yield slightly to pressure, and it will have a perfumy fragrance. Refrigerate ripe fruit in a plastic or paper bag for up to 3 days.*

A ripe mango is difficult to cut neatly because the flesh is very soft and juicy and clings to the flat seed. The simplest method is to stand the mango upright on its widest end on a cutting board. Use a sharp paring knife to cut vertically, slightly off-center, through the flesh on 1 of the flatter sides, curving around the seed. Place 1 mango half, skin side down, on a cutting board or in the palm of 1 hand. Score the flesh all the way to the skin in a checkerboard pattern, cutting to, but not through, the outer skin. Carefully push up the skin side to expose cubes of flesh. Then cut the mango cubes from the peel. For the center section, slice off the skin, then cut the flesh away from the seed or enjoy the juicy, sweet center over the sink!

MAIN COURSES

THE ACIDITY OF WINE adds its vibrant character to savory dishes. Grains and pastas, which are bland in their own right, are a natural for sauces made with spirits, and hearty beans welcome the addition of a full-bodied wine.

Wine, of course, is a customary ingredient in risotto, where it contributes to the creamy texture and brings its character to this elegant Italian dish. When simmered with rice, beans, and tomatoes, a full-bodied red mellows. In the Tomato Pie (*page 126*),

Pinot Noir lends a subtle hand as it enhances the rich flavors of plum tomatoes, which have been reduced to a thick sauce. And Cabernet adds its unmistakable presence to a rustic Vegetarian Cassoulet (*page 162*), to serve as a hearty one-dish meal.

Linguine with Morels and Asparagus (*page 140*), the most elegant dish in this chapter, calls for cream combined with Cognac or dry sherry, while Marsala makes a mushroom sauce just sweet enough to pair well with a variety of earthy mushrooms in the Bow Ties with Marsala-Mushroom Sauce (*page 150*).

Many of these *spirited vegetarian* recipes were inspired by my travels to Italy, whose great cooks traditionally add wine to pasta sauces. One less well-known dish, Spaghetti di Vino with Beets (*page 154*), combines plummy red wine with spaghetti. I've also added beets, a truly divine surprise.

Here you'll find several wine-enriched sauces that will add panache to many creations in this book as well as to favorite dishes already in your repertoire. I'm especially fond of the Roasted Red Bell Pepper Sauce (*page 170*), which always gets raves from guests both for its unique flavor and vivid hue.

Accompanying the recipes in this chapter, you'll find my suggestions for wine pairings, which will surely offer synergy and harmony, as well as pleasure, to the spirited experience. ❧

Gingered Squash Risotto
with Glazed Pecans and Fried Sage

Risotto is the perfect icebreaker when company gathers in the kitchen. While you toss a salad, draft your guests to take a turn stirring the rice. In the process, it will absorb about 4 times its own volume in liquid, allowing the semisweet and fruity Riesling to offer a delicate yet complex quality to the elegant dish. Make the Glazed Pecans and Fried Sage garnishes in advance.

MAKES 6 TO 8 SERVINGS
WINE PAIRING: RIESLING

5	cups vegetable stock (see page 18), or as needed		1	cup coarsely chopped radicchio (see Tips, page 114)
3	tablespoons unsalted butter, divided		½	cup dried cranberries
2	cups acorn squash (or other orange-fleshed winter squash) in ¼" dice (see Tips, page 131)		¼	cup freshly grated Gruyère cheese (see Tips, page 114)
1	cup sliced cremini mushrooms (about 3 ounces)		½	teaspoon minced fresh ginger, or to taste
½	cup finely chopped onion		½	teaspoon freshly ground pepper, or to taste
¼	cup finely chopped shallots		¼	teaspoon freshly grated nutmeg
1½	cups Arborio rice (see Tips, page 114)			Glazed Pecans and Fried Sage (*page 115*) for garnish
½	cup Riesling or other medium-bodied, high-acid, semisweet white wine			

Bring the vegetable stock to a simmer in a small saucepan. Cover and adjust the heat to maintain a simmer.

Melt 2 tablespoons of the butter in a large sauté pan over medium-high heat. Add the squash, mushrooms, onion, and shallots. Cook, stirring occasionally,

(continued)

until the vegetables are almost tender, about 12 minutes. Add the remaining 1 tablespoon of butter and stir until melted. Add the rice and stir to coat with the butter.

Add the wine and simmer to evaporate. Pour ½ cup of the simmering stock into the rice (maintain a cooking temperature high enough so that the hot broth continues bubbling after it is added to the rice). Cook, stirring constantly, until the stock is absorbed, about 2 minutes. Continue adding the stock, ½ cup at a time, stirring until it is mostly absorbed and evaporated before adding more. (It may not be necessary to use all the stock, or more may be needed.) Cook the risotto, adding stock as needed, until the rice is tender but still firm, about 20 to 25 minutes.

When adding the last ½ cup of vegetable stock, reduce the heat to low. Then add the remaining ingredients, except the garnish, and stir until the radicchio is wilted. Taste and adjust the seasoning.

Garnish the servings with Glazed Pecans and Fried Sage.

TIPS | *Arborio rice is an Italian short-grain, high-starch rice used in risotto, Spanish paella, and rice puddings because the grains impart a creamy texture.*

The most common variety of radicchio (also known as Italian chicory) has tender but firm, slightly bitter-tasting, burgundy-red leaves with white ribs that grow to form a small, round, loose head. Store radicchio for up to 1 week in a plastic bag in the refrigerator.

Gruyère cheese is a cow's milk cheese with a rich, sweet, nutty flavor and a pale yellow color. Buy the aged Swiss or French variety that is cut into wedges from large wheels rather than processed Gruyère.

Glazed Pecans

2	tablespoons unsalted butter		½	teaspoon salt
2	tablespoons light corn syrup		2	cups pecan halves
1	tablespoon water			

Preheat the oven to 250°F. Line a jelly roll pan with foil and lightly coat it with cooking spray.

Melt the butter in a small nonstick saucepan over medium heat. Stir in the corn syrup, water, and salt. Bring to a boil. Remove the pan from the heat. Add the pecans and stir until completely coated.

Spread the nuts on the prepared pan. Bake, stirring occasionally, for about 60 minutes, or until lightly browned and dry.

Fried Sage

	Extra-virgin olive oil, as needed	Fine-textured salt for sprinkling
6–8	whole large, fresh sage leaves	

Pour ½" of oil into a small saucepan or skillet and heat over medium-high heat. When a drop of water sizzles when sprinkled into the pan, add the sage leaves. Fry for about 15 seconds, turning frequently with a slotted spoon or tongs. (The secret is keeping the oil at a temperature that will fry the sage leaves but not brown them, which will turn the flavor bitter.)

Transfer the leaves to a paper towel–lined plate. The leaves will become crisp as they cool. Sprinkle lightly with fine-textured salt.

Saffron Risotto with Vegetables in Curry Cream Sauce

This aromatic risotto plays the unique flavor of saffron against the butteriness of Chardonnay in a colorful, elegant, and creamy dish. Because this recipe has 2 distinct elements, it's perfect for a cooking duo: one making the risotto, the other preparing the vegetables.

Makes 4 servings
Wine pairing: Gewürztraminer

For the risotto

4	cups vegetable stock (see page 18)	¼	cup finely chopped onion
	Generous pinch of saffron threads, crushed (see Tips, page 118)	1	cup Arborio rice
		½	cup Chardonnay or other rich, full-bodied white wine
1	tablespoon hot water		Dash of salt, or to taste
1	tablespoon unsalted butter		Dash of ground white pepper, or to taste

For the vegetables

1	tablespoon canola oil	½	teaspoon lemon zest
2	carrots, cut into ¼" dice	1	cup heavy cream
1	red bell pepper, cut into ¼" dice	1	cup frozen baby peas, thawed
¼	cup minced shallots		Salt and ground white pepper to taste
1	tablespoon curry powder (see Tips, page 118)		
1	teaspoon minced fresh ginger		Sprigs of fresh cilantro and finely chopped fresh chives for garnish
¼	cup Chardonnay or other rich, full-bodied white wine		

To make the risotto, bring the vegetable stock to a simmer in a small saucepan.

Combine the saffron and hot water in a small bowl and set aside to soften.

Melt the butter in a large nonstick skillet over medium-high heat. Add the onion and cook, stirring occasionally, until the onion is translucent, about 5 minutes. Add the rice and stir to coat with the butter.

Add the wine and simmer until it evaporates. Stir in the saffron mixture.

Pour ½ cup of the simmering stock into the rice (maintain a cooking temperature high enough so that the hot broth continues bubbling after it is added to the rice). Cook, stirring constantly, until the stock is absorbed, about 2 minutes. Continue adding stock ½ cup at a time, stirring until it is mostly absorbed and evaporated before adding more. Cook the risotto, adding stock as needed, until the rice is tender but still firm, about 25 minutes. Stir in the salt and pepper. Taste and adjust the seasoning. Remove from the heat and cover to keep warm.

To prepare the vegetables, heat the oil in a large sauté pan over medium-high heat. Add the carrots and bell pepper and cook, stirring constantly, for about 5 minutes, or until crisp-tender. Add the shallots and continue to cook, stirring constantly, until the vegetables are tender, about 5 more minutes. Stir in the curry powder and ginger, stirring constantly for about 30 seconds. Then, stir in the wine and lemon zest and simmer for about 1 minute. Add the cream and simmer, cooking occasionally, until the sauce is reduced by about one-third. Add the peas, salt, and pepper, stirring gently until the peas are warm. Taste and adjust the seasoning.

(continued)

To serve, top individual servings of risotto with the vegetables and sauce. Or, for each serving, form the risotto into a cylinder. Unmold onto the plate and top with the vegetables and sauce. Garnish with cilantro sprigs, and scatter the plate with chives.

TIPS | ❀ *Saffron, the red stigmas of small purple crocuses, is the world's most expensive spice. Each flower provides only 3 stigmas, which must be handpicked; it takes 14,000 of these to equal 1 ounce of saffron. That's more than 200,000 in 1 pound. And only 5 to 7 pounds of saffron can be produced from 1 acre of land. There is no substitute for its exquisite flavor and earthy aroma.*

Purchase whole saffron threads; powdered saffron loses its flavor more readily and can easily be adulterated with less expensive powders such as turmeric. Heat releases the flavor and liquid releases the characteristic yellow color, so crush the threads between your fingers, and then soak them in hot water, milk, or alcoholic liquid (depending on the recipe) for about 10 minutes before using. Store saffron in an airtight container in a cool, dark place for up to 6 months.

❀ *Curry powder is a blend of many herbs and spices that varies according to the region of India and the taste of the cook. Ready-made standard curry powders are quite mild; imported brands, often called Madras, are usually more complex. To eliminate the raw taste, sauté it in butter or oil before adding to a dish. It quickly loses its pungency, so purchase it in small quantities and store airtight in a dark, dry place for up to 3 months.*

Rice with Sun-Dried Tomatoes and Beans

This dish is often a delicious destination for my leftover brown or white rice. I like to stuff the completed rice mixture into assorted red, yellow, and green bell peppers (caps removed and centers hollowed out) and sprinkle the filling with Parmesan cheese. I arrange the peppers in a roasting pan with 1/2" of water and bake at 375°F for about 45 minutes, or until the peppers are tender.

MAKES 6 SERVINGS | VEGAN RECIPE (*if Parmesan cheese garnish is omitted*)
WINE PAIRING: SANGIOVESE

1	tablespoon olive oil	1	tablespoon finely chopped fresh basil or 1/2 teaspoon dried basil
1	cup finely chopped onion		
2	cloves garlic, minced	1	tablespoon finely chopped fresh oregano or 1/2 teaspoon dried oregano
1 1/2	cups cooked long-grain brown rice		
1	can (15 ounces) diced tomatoes	1	teaspoon sugar
1	can (15 ounces) kidney beans, drained and rinsed	1/8	teaspoon red-pepper flakes, or to taste
1/2	cup Cabernet Sauvignon or other full-bodied red wine	1/4	teaspoon salt, or to taste
1/2	cup finely chopped oil-packed sun-dried tomatoes, drained well	1/4	teaspoon pepper, or to taste
			Freshly shredded Parmesan cheese for garnish
1/2	cup dried currants		

Heat the oil in a large skillet over medium-high heat. Add the onion and cook, stirring occasionally, until translucent, about 5 minutes. Add the garlic and stir constantly for about 1 minute. Reduce the heat to medium, then stir in the remaining ingredients, except the garnish. Cover and simmer, stirring occasionally, until the liquid is absorbed, about 20 minutes. Taste and adjust the seasoning. Garnish the servings with Parmesan.

POLENTA TRIANGLES

Authentic polenta (not the instant variety), an Italian cook's version of cornmeal, is ideal for making this dish. Supermarket cornmeal will do, but look for the "stone-ground" variety, which is best for both flavor and texture. Also be sure to use top-quality Parmesan cheese, such as Parmigiano-Reggiano.

This is one dish where it's important to plan ahead. Start the polenta at least 1 hour before serving, because it needs to firm up in the refrigerator before being browned in a skillet, grilled, or broiled. You can cut the polenta into thinner wedges to serve as an appetizer or first course.

For serving as either a main dish or an appetizer, top with any of the following:

❀ Tomato-Caper Sauce (*page 34*)

❀ Roasted Vegetables (*page 123*) topped with Sangiovese Tomato Sauce (*page 166*) or Roasted Red Bell Pepper Sauce (*page 170*)

❀ Ruby Port–Glazed Portobello Mushrooms (*page 124*)

❀ Sangiovese Tomato Sauce (*page 166*)

❀ Spicy Merlot Marinara (*page 168*)

❀ Roasted Red Bell Pepper Sauce (*page 170*)

MAKES 6 SERVINGS

2	tablespoons unsalted butter	½	cup yellow cornmeal
½	cup finely chopped red onion	¼	cup freshly grated Parmesan cheese
¾	cup Chardonnay or other rich, full-bodied white wine	¼	teaspoon freshly ground pepper
1	cup water		Olive oil for brushing
¼	teaspoon salt		

Melt the butter in a medium sauté pan over medium heat. Add the onion and cook, stirring occasionally, until translucent, about 5 minutes. Stir in the wine, water, and salt. As soon as it begins to simmer, slowly add the cornmeal, whisking or stirring constantly to prevent lumps. Reduce the heat to low and cook, stirring almost constantly, until the mixture is a smooth, creamy paste, about 10 to 15 minutes. (The polenta is done when it starts to pull away from the sides of the pan.) Stir in the Parmesan and pepper.

Evenly spread the mixture in a lightly oiled 9" pie plate. Refrigerate until firm, at least 1 hour or overnight. (When the polenta is cool, cover with plastic wrap.)

When ready to serve, lightly brush the surface of the polenta with olive oil. Halve the polenta and cut each half into 3 triangles. Heat a large nonstick skillet over medium-high heat. Arrange the triangles, oiled side down, in a single layer and lightly brush the tops with olive oil. Cook until lightly browned and thoroughly heated, about 2 minutes per side. If you prefer, the triangles can be cooked on a stove-top grill pan over medium-high heat or broiled on a baking sheet for about 2 to 3 minutes per side.

Polenta Pizza

I created this recipe quite by accident one afternoon. Earlier in the day, I had retested my polenta recipe, and the pan was cooling in the refrigerator. A friend unexpectedly stopped by, so I offered to make a light lunch. Here's the mouthwatering result, perfectly paired with Pinot Grigio, which is always delicious with basil pesto.

MAKES 6 SERVINGS
WINE PAIRING: PINOT GRIGIO

	One 9" pie plate of polenta (*page 120*)		Dash of salt
2	tablespoons Basil Pesto (*page 36*)		Dash of freshly ground pepper
2	plum tomatoes, thinly sliced	¼	cup freshly shredded Parmesan cheese (see Tips)

Preheat the oven to 400°F.

Spread the surface of the polenta with the pesto. Arrange the tomato slices in overlapping concentric circles. Sprinkle with salt and pepper, then top with Parmesan.

Bake for about 15 minutes, or until the Parmesan is melted. To serve, cut into 6 wedges.

TIPS | ❧ *The best-quality Parmesan cheese is northern Italy's Parmigiano-Reggiano. It's aged 3 to 4 years, which lends it a firm, granular texture and complex flavor as compared with domestic varieties, which are aged for only about 1 year. The imported cheese also melts beautifully.* Warning: *The commercially packaged, pregrated Parmesan that is sold unrefrigerated is loaded with preservatives and is overly salty. Instead, buy Parmesan in blocks and use a hand grater or food processor to grate just before using. Or, purchase freshly grated Parmesan at a cheese shop or deli. Sealed in a tightly closed container, grated Parmesan will keep in the refrigerator for up to 1 week. Wrapped tightly in plastic wrap and refrigerated, a block of Parmesan will keep for up to 6 weeks. The cheese can be frozen; however, the flavor and texture will deteriorate.*

ROASTED VEGETABLES

Roasting intensifies the flavors of vegetables and brings out their natural sweetness. The vegetables can be tossed with the oil and herbs up to 2 hours before roasting. Cover and let stand at room temperature, then roast just before serving. I use this robust and tasty medley in one of my favorite main courses, piled over Polenta Triangles (page 120) and topped with Sangiovese Tomato Sauce (page 166) or Roasted Red Bell Pepper Sauce (page 170).

MAKES 6 SERVINGS | VEGAN RECIPE (*if cheese garnish is omitted*)

1/3	cup olive oil	1	medium eggplant, peeled and cut into 1/2"-wide wedges
4	cloves garlic, minced	2	portobello mushrooms, black ribs removed and discarded, caps cut into 1/2"-thick slices
2	teaspoons finely chopped fresh oregano		
1	teaspoon finely chopped fresh rosemary	1	red bell pepper, cut into 1/2"-wide strips
1	teaspoon finely chopped fresh thyme	1/2	red onion, cut into 1/2"-wide wedges
1/4	teaspoon freshly ground pepper		Freshly shredded Parmesan cheese or crumbled feta cheese for garnish
1/4	teaspoon salt		

Preheat the oven to 425°F. Line a large jelly roll pan with foil.

Stir together the oil, garlic, oregano, rosemary, thyme, pepper, and salt in a large bowl. Add all the vegetables and toss to coat.

Spread the vegetables in a single layer on the prepared pan. Bake, turning the vegetables occasionally, for 15 to 20 minutes, or until they are tender and lightly browned.

Garnish the servings with Parmesan or feta cheese.

Ruby Port–Glazed Portobello Mushrooms

My favorite presentation is to top bowls of fettuccine with Spicy Merlot Marinara (page 168) or Roasted Red Bell Pepper Sauce (page 170), and then I add these meaty mushrooms as the crowning glory. For a special lunch, roll the sliced mushrooms and onions in a pita spread with Basil Pesto (page 36) and chèvre; add some Roasted Red Bell Pepper Sauce (page 170) for color. Or, call on the aromatic mushrooms to fill an omelette, to flavor bruschetta, or to serve with Polenta Triangles (page 120). If you prefer, you can cook the mushrooms whole and serve Cranberry Margarita Relish (page 43) on the side to brighten up the plate.

If you don't have Ruby Port on hand, you can substitute 1 cup Red Zinfandel with 1 tablespoon sugar added for sweetness.

MAKES 4 SERVINGS
WINE PAIRING: SHIRAZ

2	tablespoons olive oil	4	large portobello mushrooms, ribs removed and discarded, caps cut into ½"-wide slices (see Tips)
1	large sweet onion, thinly sliced (see Tips, page 71)		
1	cup Ruby Port		Dash of salt (see Tips)
2	tablespoons unsalted butter		Dash of freshly ground pepper
2	cloves garlic, minced		

Heat the oil in a large skillet over medium heat. Add the onion and cook, stirring occasionally, until tender and lightly browned, about 20 minutes. Add the wine, butter, and garlic and stir until the butter is melted. Place the mushrooms in the pan in a single layer. Cook, using tongs to turn the mushrooms occasionally, until they are thoroughly done but not mushy, about 8 to 10 minutes.

To serve, top the mushrooms with the onion and wine sauce and sprinkle lightly with a dash of salt and pepper.

TIPS | ❧ *Portobellos are mushrooms up to 6" in diameter that achieve their size through a long growing cycle. In the process, some of the mushrooms' moisture evaporates, concentrating and enriching the flavor, which creates a dense, meaty texture. Slice off the woody stems and remove the black gills with a spoon before using.*

❧ *In my own cooking, I prefer to use sea salt, which is made from evaporated seawater. It has a fresher and fuller flavor, so usually, less is needed. You can purchase sea salt in many supermarkets as well as in natural foods stores. Fine sea salt can be used just like ordinary table salt. Coarse sea salt can be ground in a salt mill. (Make sure the mill has a stainless steel or other noncorrosive mechanism.) Sel gris, a specialty variety, is gray in color and slightly moist; use it to season foods while cooking. Fleur de sel, another specialty salt, is used to add flavor at the table. You'll find these salts in gourmet shops.*

TOMATO PIE

This rustic dish calls for an earthy red wine, such as Pinot Noir. For ease of preparation, use a store-bought pie crust, which you'll find in the freezer section of most supermarkets. Or try my Basic Pie Crust, which takes just minutes to prepare using a food processor. This pie can be made early in the day and reheated in the microwave. Or you can cut it into thin slices to serve as a room-temperature appetizer or first course. Thank you, Jane, for sharing this recipe.

MAKES ONE 9" PIE (*6 servings*)
WINE PAIRING: SANGIOVESE

2	tablespoons olive oil	½	teaspoon freshly ground pepper, or to taste
¾	cup finely chopped onion	1	(9") store-bought frozen pie crust or Basic Pie Crust (*opposite page*)
4	cloves garlic, minced		
1½	pounds plum tomatoes (8 to 10), cut into ½" cubes (about 4 cups)	½	cup freshly shredded Parmesan cheese
½	cup Pinot Noir or other medium-bodied, earthy red wine	1	can (2¼ ounces) sliced black olives, drained
¼	cup finely chopped fresh basil or 1 teaspoon dried basil	1	cup (4 ounces) finely shredded mozzarella cheese
3	cups stemmed and coarsely chopped fresh spinach		

Preheat the oven to 350°F.

Heat the oil in a large sauté pan over medium heat. Add the onion and cook, stirring occasionally, until translucent, about 5 minutes. Add the garlic and stir constantly for about 1 minute. Add the tomatoes, wine, and dried basil (if using). When the liquid begins to bubble, reduce the heat to medium-low. Cook, uncovered, stirring occasionally until the liquid is absorbed and evaporated, about 20 minutes. Stir in the spinach, fresh basil (if using), and pepper. Taste and adjust the seasoning.

Pierce the bottom of the crust in several places with a fork and bake in the lowest third of the oven for 10 to 15 minutes, or until the crust is firm but not browned.

Spread the Parmesan in the partially baked crust. Top with an even layer of the tomato mixture. Add a layer of olives and top with the mozzarella cheese.

Bake in the lowest third of the preheated oven for about 35 minutes, or until the filling is set and the edges of the crust are lightly browned. Let stand on a rack for about 10 minutes before slicing into wedges for serving.

BASIC PIE CRUST

The egg enriches this crust, giving it less flakiness but more flavor and body than a typical pie crust. This bakes well at 350°F, but follow whatever recipe you're using.

MAKES ONE 9" CRUST

1¼	cups all-purpose flour	¼	teaspoon salt
½	cup (1 stick) cold unsalted butter, cut into about 6 pieces	1	egg

Combine the flour, butter, and salt in a food processor. Pulse until the mixture looks like cornmeal. Add the egg and process just until the dough holds together to form a ball.

On a cutting board, flatten the dough between 2 sheets of waxed paper. Using a rolling pin, roll outward from the center to form an 11" round. Remove the top waxed-paper covering, turn the dough out into a 9" pie plate, and remove the second sheet of waxed paper. Use your fingers to press the crust firmly into the sides of the plate. Trim the dough to a ½" overhang all around and then tuck it under itself around the edge of the plate. Crimp the edges with a fork or with your fingers.

CANNELLINI BEAN BOURGUIGNONNE

Bourguignonne means "as prepared in Burgundy," the area in eastern France noted for its superb wines. Standing deepens and mellows the flavors of this hearty peasant stew, so if possible, prepare the dish an hour or so before serving. It also will keep in a covered container in the refrigerator for up to 2 days and is delicious reheated. Serve the chunky, aromatic stew in bowls along with crusty bread, which you can use to scoop up every last drop of the hearty sauce.

MAKES 4 SERVINGS | VEGAN RECIPE
WINE PAIRING: CHARDONNAY

3	tablespoons olive oil, divided	2	bay leaves (see Tips)
¾	cup finely chopped onion	1	cup Pinot Noir or other medium-bodied, earthy red wine
2	cloves garlic, minced	1	can (15 ounces) cannellini beans, drained and rinsed (see Tips)
1¼	cups water		
1	can (6 ounces) tomato paste	3	cups sliced cremini mushrooms (about 8 ounces)
1	large russet potato, peeled and cut into ¾" cubes	¼	teaspoon salt, or to taste
1	large carrot, halved lengthwise and cut into ¼"-thick slices	¼	teaspoon freshly ground pepper, or to taste
1	tablespoon finely chopped fresh thyme or 1 teaspoon dried thyme		

Heat 1 tablespoon of the oil in a large sauté pan over medium-high heat. Add the onion and cook, stirring occasionally, until translucent, about 5 minutes. Add the garlic and stir constantly for about 1 minute.

Whisk together the water and half of the tomato paste in a small bowl, then add to the sauté pan. Stir in the potato, carrot, thyme, and bay leaves. When the liquid comes to a boil, reduce the heat to medium, cover, and cook until the potato and carrot begin to turn tender but are not thoroughly cooked, about 20 minutes.

Whisk together the wine and the remaining tomato paste in a small bowl. Add to the pan. Stir in the cannellini beans and increase the heat to high. When the liquid returns to a boil, reduce the heat to medium. Cook, uncovered, until the potato and carrot are tender and the sauce is reduced by about one-half and thickened, about 10 minutes.

Meanwhile, heat the remaining 2 tablespoons of oil in a medium nonstick skillet over medium heat. Add the mushrooms and cook, stirring occasionally, until tender but not browned, about 5 minutes. Remove from the heat.

Remove and discard the bay leaves from the stew. Stir in the mushrooms, salt, and pepper. Taste and adjust the seasoning.

TIPS | ❦ *Rosemary, thyme, oregano, savory, sage, marjoram, and bay leaf are considered to be the "robust herbs," with tough leaves that are resistant to cold weather and to heat—both from the sun and cooking. They are strong in aroma and hearty in flavor, so add them early in the cooking process to give them time to mellow and blend in with the other ingredients. Add tender fresh herbs, such as basil, cilantro, dill, and parsley, toward the end of the cooking time, or sprinkle them on top of the completed dish.*

❦ *Cannellini beans are large, white Italian kidney beans. In most supermarkets, they can be found either with the canned beans or with the Italian products.*

Acorn Squash and Red Lentils with Toasted Walnuts

When fall brings its bright foliage, it's time to cook acorn squash. This dish is both homey and elegant, ideal for a weeknight family meal, yet also appropriate for guests. I always accompany it with greens in a creamy dressing, bread from my favorite artisan bakery, light-bodied and aromatic Beaujolais, and chocolate (of course!) for dessert. Chocolate-Cherry Bread Pudding with Sherry Cream (page 176) somehow always seems just right.

Makes 4 servings | Vegan recipe
Wine pairing: Beaujolais

1	tablespoon canola oil
1	red bell pepper, coarsely chopped
1	carrot, coarsely chopped
½	cup coarsely chopped red onion
1	tablespoon curry powder
2	cups vegetable stock (see page 18)
½	cup Riesling or other medium-bodied, high-acid, semisweet white wine

1	acorn squash, halved, seeded, peeled, and cut into 1" chunks (about 3 cups), see Tips
¾	cup red lentils (see Tips)
⅛	teaspoon salt, or to taste
¼	teaspoon freshly ground pepper, or to taste
	Coarsely chopped toasted walnuts (see Tips, page 73) for garnish

Heat the oil in a large sauté pan over medium heat. Add the bell pepper, carrot, and onion. Cook, stirring occasionally, for 10 minutes, or until the vegetables begin to soften but are not browned. Add the curry powder and stir constantly for about 30 seconds.

Stir in the vegetable stock, wine, squash, and lentils. Increase the heat to medium-high. When the liquid begins to bubble, reduce the heat to low. Cover and cook for about 20 minutes, or until the squash and lentils are tender. (Check occasionally as the dish cooks and add water if necessary.) Stir in the salt and pepper. Taste and adjust the seasoning.

Spoon the dish into a large serving bowl or into individual shallow bowls and garnish with walnuts.

TIPS | ❦ *Winter squash comes in countless varieties. All have a dense, sweet flesh and thick skin, which allows them to be stored for 3 to 4 weeks in a cool, dry place. A vegetable peeler is no match for the thick skin, so follow this procedure: Pierce the skin several times with a fork. Heat the squash in the microwave oven on high power for about 2 minutes, then let it stand for about 2 more minutes. Slice off the 2 ends and cut the squash in half near the center. Place each half on its widest cut side and use a knife or vegetable peeler to remove the peel in strips, working from the top to the bottom.*

❦ *Lentils are tiny legume seeds that were dried as soon as they ripened. All lentils have an earthy, almost nutty flavor. The most common variety is brown lentils, which retain their shape after cooking. Dried red lentils (sometimes called Egyptian lentils) are smaller and orange. They cook quickly, fall apart, and turn bright yellow during cooking.*

Store lentils at room temperature in a tightly closed container for up to 1 year. Before using, rinse in a colander to remove dust; pick through them and discard any shriveled lentils or bits of gravel.

Unlike other dried beans, lentils don't need soaking before cooking.

You can add garlic, herbs, and spices to the lentil cooking liquid. Avoid adding salt and acidic ingredients, such as tomatoes, until the lentils are cooked. Adding these ingredients increases the cooking time necessary for the lentils to soften.

ASPARAGUS-CASHEW STIR-FRY

Serve this stir-fry with its gingery sweet sauce over rice or thin Chinese wheat-flour noodles. Feel free to substitute other vegetables (up to 5 cups total), such as coarsely chopped bok choy, coarsely shredded Chinese cabbage, and sliced mushrooms. If you use vegetables of varying consistencies, begin cooking the firmest first, and add the tender vegetables last. No need for a traditional wok; a sauté pan is just fine.

MAKES 4 SERVINGS | VEGAN RECIPE
WINE PAIRING: RIESLING

For the sauce

2	tablespoons cold water
2	tablespoons cornstarch
1½	cups vegetable stock (see page 18)
3	tablespoons soy sauce
2	tablespoons dry sherry
1	tablespoon minced fresh ginger
2	teaspoons toasted (Asian) sesame oil (see Tips)
¼	teaspoon red-pepper flakes, or to taste
⅛	teaspoon ground white pepper, or to taste

For the stir-fry

2	tablespoons canola oil
2	cups asparagus in 2" lengths
1	red bell pepper, cut into 2" × ¼" strips
1	cup sliced mushrooms
4	scallions, both white and green parts, coarsely chopped
½	cup raw whole cashews
2	cloves garlic, minced
6	ounces firm tofu, cut into ½" cubes (see Tips)
	Toasted sesame seeds (see Tips) for garnish

To make the sauce, stir together the water and cornstarch in a medium smooth. Whisk in the remaining ingredients and set aside.

To cook the stir-fry, heat the oil in a large sauté pan or wok over medium-high heat. Add the asparagus and bell pepper and stir-fry, tossing constantly, until the vegetables are crisp-tender, about 5 minutes. Add the mushrooms, scallions, and cashews and stir-fry for about 2 minutes. Add the garlic, stirring constantly for about 1 minute.

Reduce the heat to medium. Stir the sauce mixture, pour over the vegetables, and stir gently until it is thickened and bubbly, about 1 minute. Gently fold in the tofu and heat until warm. Taste and adjust the seasoning.

Serve the stir-fry over rice or noodles. Garnish with sesame seeds.

TIPS | ❧ *Buy the dark, amber-colored, toasted sesame oil made from toasted sesame seeds rather than light-colored sesame oil, which is extracted from the raw seeds and lacks the distinctive strong aroma and nutty flavor.*

❧ *Tofu, or bean curd, is made from soybeans. The texture, which you'll find labeled on the package, varies from soft to firm, depending on how much water is extracted during processing. Choose extra-firm or firm tofu if you want it to hold a sliced or diced shape. Soft tofu is better suited for dips, sauces, and puddings, where a creamy consistency is desired.*

❧ *Toasting gives sesame seeds a slightly crispy texture and a nutty flavor. Put the seeds in a dry skillet over medium-high heat and toss constantly until they are lightly browned, about 3 to 5 minutes.*

RED WINE RATATOUILLE

I love having ratatouille on hand! It's an easy do-ahead recipe to multiply for a crowd, and the flavors blend as it stands in the refrigerator for up to 5 days. Ratatouille is a meal in itself with rice or with good French bread for mopping up the juices, which are peppery from the addition of Shiraz. Ratatouille is also delicious in pita sandwiches, as a filling for omelettes, or spooned over a baked potato and topped with shredded Cheddar cheese. Mound it over plates of pasta, such as cavatappi, for a substantial meal.

MAKES 6 CUPS (*6 servings*) | VEGAN RECIPE
WINE PAIRING: SYRAH

¼	cup olive oil	½	cup Shiraz or other full-bodied, ripe-jammy red wine
1	large onion, quartered and cut into ¼"-thick slices	3	tomatoes, cut into ½" cubes
4	cloves garlic, minced	1	tablespoon sugar
1	eggplant (about 1½ pounds), peeled and cut into ½" cubes (about 6 cups), see Tips	2	tablespoons finely chopped fresh basil (see Tips) or 2 teaspoons dried basil
2	cups green beans in 2" lengths	1	tablespoon finely chopped fresh oregano (see Tips) or 1 teaspoon dried oregano
1	green bell pepper, coarsely chopped	½	teaspoon salt, or to taste
1	red bell pepper, coarsely chopped	½	teaspoon freshly ground pepper, or to taste
1	can (15 ounces) tomato sauce		

Heat the oil in a Dutch oven over medium heat. Add the onion and cook, stirring occasionally, until tender, about 8 minutes. Add the garlic and stir constantly for about 1 minute.

Reduce the heat to low. Add the eggplant, green beans, and bell peppers. Cover and cook, stirring occasionally, for 30 minutes.

Add the remaining ingredients, cover, and continue to cook, stirring occasionally, until the beans are tender, about 30 minutes. Taste and adjust the seasoning.

If time permits, let the ratatouille stand, covered, for 20 minutes before serving. Serve warm or at room temperature.

TIPS | ❧ *Select an eggplant with firm, taut skin, glossy color, and flesh that bounces back when lightly pressed. Store it for up to 1 week in a plastic bag in the refrigerator; keep the stem on until just before using. The peel of a young eggplant is edible, so it is not necessary to remove it before cooking; peel it if the eggplant is very large and mature or for the sake of appearance.*

❧ *To store tender fresh herbs (parsley, basil, cilantro, dill, and tarragon), first trim the stems (unless the roots are still attached). Wrap the ends in a moist paper towel and refrigerate in a sealed bag. Or place the bunch, stems down, in a glass of water and cover with a plastic bag, securing the bag to the glass with a rubber band; store this on the top shelf of the refrigerator (the warmest part) and change the water every 2 days. With proper storage, most fresh tender herbs will last for about 5 days. For the best flavor, use within 2 or 3 days.*

To store hardy, robust fresh herbs (thyme, oregano, marjoram, rosemary, and sage), wrap the stem ends in a damp paper towel, put the herbs in a plastic bag, and refrigerate, unsealed, for up to 2 weeks. Just before using, wash fresh herbs in cool water, and then dry with paper towels or in a salad spinner.

TEQUILA-BRAISED KALE

*Many thanks to my cooking class culinary assistant and vegetarian friend Lisa Genis for intro-
ducing me to dinosaur (or black) kale, which is quite similar to the Tuscan variety, and for sharing
this unusual recipe she created. Robust kale, with its bitter edge, partners well with chickpeas. It's
also a great mate for couscous (see Tips), which I prepare according to the package directions to
use as a base for the braised kale.*

MAKES 4 SERVINGS | VEGAN RECIPE
WINE PAIRING: PINOT GRIGIO

½	cup dry-packed sun-dried tomatoes	2	cloves garlic, thinly sliced
1	cup boiling water	1	bunch dinosaur or curly kale, stemmed (if necessary) and coarsely chopped (about 8 cups), see Tips
⅓	cup tequila		
2	tablespoons white wine vinegar	1	can (15 ounces) chickpeas, drained and rinsed
2	tablespoons olive oil		
1	medium sweet onion, halved lengthwise and cut into ¼"-thick slices (about 1 cup), see Tips, page 71	2	tablespoons fresh lime juice
		½	teaspoon salt, or to taste
		¼	teaspoon freshly ground pepper, or to taste
1	teaspoon whole cumin seeds		

Combine the sun-dried tomatoes and boiling water in a small bowl. Soak the
tomatoes for about 10 minutes, or until softened. Drain, reserving the liquid. Use
kitchen scissors to cut the tomatoes into matchstick strips.

To make the braising liquid, combine the tequila, the vinegar, and the tomato
liquid in a small bowl.

Heat the oil in a large sauté pan over medium heat. Add the onion and cook, stirring occasionally, until it just begins to soften, about 5 minutes. Add the cumin
seeds and garlic and stir constantly for about 30 seconds.

Add the kale and stir until it is coated with the oil. Add the braising liquid, tomatoes, and chickpeas. Reduce the heat to low, cover, and cook until the kale is tender, about 7 to 10 minutes for dinosaur kale (if using), or about 10 to 15 minutes for curly kale (if using). Stir in the lime juice, salt, and pepper. Taste and adjust the seasoning.

TIPS | ❧ *Couscous, sometimes called Moroccan pasta, is a tiny, beadlike pasta made from semolina flour. It is available in both white and whole wheat varieties in most supermarkets. It keeps almost indefinitely in a tightly closed container in a dark, dry place.*

❧ *Kale, a loose-leafed member of the cabbage family, is at its best during fall, winter, and early spring; it doesn't tolerate heat well and can become bitter if grown in the summer months. Choose fresh, brightly colored bunches of kale with no sign of browning or insect damage. Store in a perforated plastic bag in the refrigerator for up to 3 days; beyond that, the flavor becomes quite strong. Clean the leaves well just before using by swishing the greens in a bowl of cold water; lift the greens from the water, leaving any dirt in the bottom of the bowl, and repeat if necessary. Be sure to check both sides of the leaves because dirt can cling to the undersides. If they are more than $^1/_8"$ thick, remove and discard the tough center stalks before using.*

Tuscan Porcini Ragù with Spinach Fettuccine

This is a rich, satisfying ragù sauce, made meaty with porcini mushrooms. Judy Witts Francini, my Florentine friend who shared this recipe, spoons this sauce over polenta (page 120).

MAKES 6 SERVINGS | VEGAN RECIPE (*if Parmesan cheese garnish is omitted*)
WINE PAIRING: ITALIAN SANGIOVESE OR BARBERA

1	ounce dried porcini mushrooms (see Tips)	1	can (15 ounces) diced Italian plum tomatoes, with juice
2	cups hot, but not boiling, water	¼	teaspoon salt, or to taste
2	tablespoons olive oil	¼	teaspoon freshly ground pepper, or to taste
1	large red onion, finely chopped	12	ounces spinach fettuccine
1	carrot, finely chopped	¼	cup coarsely chopped fresh flat-leaf parsley
1	rib celery, finely chopped		Freshly ground pepper and freshly shredded Parmesan cheese for garnish
2	cloves garlic, minced		
½	cup Sangiovese or other medium-bodied, high-acid red wine		

Put the mushrooms in a small bowl. Add the hot water and soak until the mushrooms are softened, 20 to 30 minutes.

Meanwhile, heat the oil in a large sauté pan over medium heat. Add the onion, carrot, and celery. Cook, stirring occasionally, until the onion begins to caramelize, about 15 minutes. Add the garlic and stir constantly for about 1 minute. Remove the pan from the heat.

Bring a large pot of salted water to a boil over high heat.

Use a slotted spoon to remove the mushrooms from the water. Reserve the soaking liquid. Thoroughly rinse the mushrooms in a strainer, then pat dry. Halve the mushrooms if they are very large and set aside. Strain the soaking liquid through a fine-mesh strainer lined with a paper coffee filter and set aside.

Return the sauté pan to medium heat. Add the mushrooms and wine and simmer, stirring occasionally, until the liquid evaporates, about 4 minutes.

Add 1 cup of the strained mushroom-soaking liquid, the tomatoes and their juice, salt, and pepper. Bring the mixture to a boil over medium-high heat. Reduce the heat to medium. Cook, uncovered, until most of the liquid evaporates and the sauce thickens, about 10 minutes. Add more soaking liquid, if necessary.

Cook the fettuccine according to the package directions while the sauce is cooking. Drain well.

Stir the parsley into the sauce when it is done cooking. Taste and adjust the seasoning.

To serve, spoon the sauce over fettucine in individual pasta bowls. Sprinkle with pepper and garnish generously with Parmesan.

TIPS | ❧ *Porcini mushrooms, also called* cèpes, *are wild mushrooms that are found throughout the woodlands of Italy and northern Europe, where they grow beneath pine or other evergreen trees. They defy cultivation. The mushrooms have a tender, meaty texture; a rich, nutty flavor; and a woodsy scent. Fresh porcini are difficult to find. Dried porcini, found in many supermarkets and specialty markets, are a fine substitute; soften them in hot water before using.*

Linguine with Morels and Asparagus

My son has fond memories of his first experience with morels, the night we celebrated his twelfth birthday at a New York restaurant. Even then, as a very young man, he recognized that these marvelous mushrooms are a food worthy of appreciation. Morels are at their elegant best in a cream sauce, making a rich and aromatic dish to be savored by gourmands. Every spring, I look forward to cooking with fresh morels. Yet dried morels, available year-round, have a more intense flavor, which is brought out especially well when they are hydrated in sherry or brandy. Admittedly, they are pricey, but 1 ounce of dried morels swells to about 4 ounces after being reconstituted. I consider it money well-spent!

Makes 4 servings
Wine pairing: Champagne

½	cup dry sherry, Cognac, or other brandy	2	teaspoons finely chopped fresh thyme
1	ounce dried morel mushrooms (see Tips)	½	teaspoon salt, or to taste
8	ounces linguine	½	teaspoon freshly ground pepper, or to taste
2	tablespoons unsalted butter		Freshly ground pepper, freshly grated Parmesan cheese, toasted pine nuts (see Tips, page 73), and sprigs of fresh flat-leaf parsley for garnish
1	tablespoon olive oil		
1½	cups asparagus in 1" lengths		
¼	cup minced shallots		
2	cups heavy cream		

Bring the sherry to a simmer in a small, covered saucepan over medium heat. Remove from the heat and add the morels. Cover and let stand, turning the mushrooms occasionally until they are softened, about 30 to 45 minutes. Using a slotted spoon, remove the morels. Halve or quarter the large mushrooms. Reserve any remaining liquid.

Bring a large pot of salted water to a boil over high heat. Cook the linguine according to package directions.

Meanwhile, melt the butter with the oil in a large sauté pan over medium heat. Add the asparagus and cook, stirring constantly, until tender, about 5 minutes. Add the morels and shallots and stir constantly for about 3 minutes. In a small bowl, combine the cream, the remaining liquid from the mushrooms, and the thyme. Stir into the sauté pan. When the cream begins to simmer, reduce the heat to low. (Do not let the sauce come to a boil.) Simmer, uncovered, stirring constantly, until the cream is thickened and reduced by about half, about 5 minutes. Stir in the salt and pepper. Taste and adjust the seasoning. Remove from the heat.

When the linguine is done, drain it well. Return the pasta to the pot and add the sauce. Stir gently over low heat until thoroughly heated.

Serve the pasta in large, shallow bowls. Garnish with pepper, Parmesan, pine nuts, and parsley sprigs.

TIPS | *Morels are edible wild mushrooms belonging to the truffle family. The flavor is smoky, earthy, and nutty; in general, the darker brown the mushroom, the more intense the flavor. Morel mushrooms should never be eaten raw because they may cause an upset stomach. Fresh morels are available in specialty produce markets in April; the season may last through June. Store morels in a brown paper bag in the refrigerator. Before using, cut the mushrooms in half to check for worms and dirt.*

Dried morels, available year-round, have a more concentrated flavor than fresh; they must be hydrated before using in recipes.

Penne with Yams and Mushrooms

Here's the perfect dish to celebrate the return of autumn. Pair it with crusty bread and a green salad for a hearty, casual meal. It may come as a surprise that the alliance of yams and pasta is very pleasing. Tasting is believing!

MAKES 4 SERVINGS
WINE PAIRING: PINOT NOIR

1	yam (about 16 ounces), peeled and quartered
8	ounces penne
2	tablespoons olive oil
3	cups sliced cremini mushrooms (about 8 ounces)
½	red onion, cut into 2" × ¼" strips
½	red bell pepper, finely chopped
2	cloves garlic, minced
½	cup dry sherry

3	tablespoons unsalted butter
2	tablespoons finely chopped fresh sage or 1 teaspoon ground dried sage (see Tips)
¼	teaspoon salt, or to taste
¼	teaspoon freshly ground pepper, or to taste
	Freshly ground pepper, freshly shredded Parmesan cheese, and toasted walnuts (see Tips, page 73) for garnish

Bring a medium saucepan of salted water to a boil over high heat. Add the yam and cook until fork-tender, about 20 minutes. When the yam is done, drain well and cut into ½" cubes. Transfer to a bowl and cover to keep warm.

Meanwhile, bring a large pot of salted water to a boil over high heat. Cook the penne according to the package directions.

Heat the oil in a large sauté pan over medium heat. Add the mushrooms, onion, and bell pepper. Cook, stirring occasionally, until tender, about 15 minutes. Add the garlic and stir constantly for about 1 minute. Reduce the heat to low, then add the sherry. Use a wooden spoon to stir, scraping up the browned juices from the bottom of the pan.

Add the butter to the sauté pan. When it has melted, stir in the sage and the yam chunks.

When the pasta is done, drain well, reserving about ¼ cup of the cooking water. Add the drained pasta to the sauté pan and toss. Add some of the pasta water, if needed, to moisten the pasta. Add the salt and pepper. Taste and adjust the seasoning.

Serve in pasta bowls and garnish with pepper, Parmesan, and walnuts.

TIPS | *Sage is a native Mediterranean herb with narrow, oval, gray-green leaves. The pungent flavor is slightly bitter, with a musty mint taste and aroma. Wrap fresh sage in a paper towel and seal it in a plastic bag for up to 4 days. Dried sage, which comes whole, rubbed (crumbled), and ground, should be stored in a cool, dark place for no more than 6 months.*

Lasagna Rolls
with Roasted Red Bell Pepper Sauce

Lasagna doesn't need to be a major production destined to serve a big crowd. For a quickly prepared intimate dinner, roll the noodles and top them with colorful and slightly sweet, red wine–scented Roasted Red Bell Pepper Sauce. It looks as gorgeous as it tastes.

MAKES 4 SERVINGS (*2 rolls per serving*)
WINE PAIRING: CÔTES DU RHÔNE

8	lasagna noodles	¼	cup freshly grated Parmesan cheese
2	tablespoons extra-virgin olive oil	2	tablespoons finely chopped fresh basil (see Tips) or 1 teaspoon dried basil
2	cups stemmed and finely shredded fresh spinach, preferably salad (baby) spinach		
2½	cups finely chopped mushrooms (about 8 ounces)	½	teaspoon salt, or to taste
2	carrots, finely shredded	½	teaspoon freshly ground pepper, or to taste
¼	cup finely chopped onion	¾	cup Roasted Red Bell Pepper Sauce (*page 170*)
2	cloves garlic, minced		
1	carton (15 ounces) ricotta cheese (1½ cups)		Toasted pine nuts (see Tips, page 73) and sprigs of fresh basil for garnish

Preheat the oven to 350°F.

Bring a large pot of salted water to a boil over high heat. Cook the lasagna noodles according to the package directions.

Meanwhile, heat the oil in a large sauté pan over medium-high heat. Add the spinach, mushrooms, carrots, onion, and garlic. Cook, stirring occasionally, until tender, about 5 minutes. Remove from the heat. Stir in the ricotta cheese, Parmesan, basil, salt, and pepper.

When the noodles are done, drain well. Rinse with cool water and drain again. Place the noodles on a flat surface and spread each with about 3 rounded table-spoons of the filling. Roll up each noodle and place seam-side down in a lightly oiled 9" × 9" baking dish. (At this point, the lasagna rolls can be covered with plastic wrap and refrigerated for up to 1 day.)

Spread the sauce over the lasagna rolls. Bake in the preheated oven for 20 minutes, or until thoroughly heated.

(Or, arrange the lasagna rolls with sauce in a microwaveable dish; heat in the microwave oven on high for about 2 minutes, turning halfway through, or until the rolls are thoroughly heated.)

Garnish the lasagna rolls with pine nuts and basil sprigs.

TIPS | ❧ *When cutting fresh herbs, use a sharp chef's knife. It's important to cut the herbs cleanly rather than crushing or bruising them. Some cooks prefer to snip herbs with kitchen scissors, which takes longer but prevents bruising.*

❧ *Pine nuts, also called* **pignoli,** *are the seeds from the cones of several varieties of pine trees. Their natural oil turns rancid very quickly, so they should be refrigerated for no more than 1 month or frozen for up to 6 months in a tightly closed container. Toasting will bring out their nutty sweetness (see Tips, page 73).*

FETTUCCINE WITH CREMINI MUSHROOMS

You won't miss the heavy cream sauce once you try this version of pasta primavera, which calls on tasty mushrooms and the first tender asparagus of spring. The meal is complete with a lightly dressed green salad, crusty Italian bread, and a crisp, light Pinot Grigio.

MAKES 4 SERVINGS
WINE PAIRING: PINOT GRIGIO

8	ounces fettuccine	$\frac{1}{4}$	cup coarsely chopped fresh flat-leaf parsley (see Tips)
2	tablespoons unsalted butter		
2	tablespoons olive oil	2	tablespoons coarsely chopped fresh basil
4	cups sliced cremini mushrooms (about 12 ounces)	$\frac{1}{2}$	cup freshly grated Parmesan cheese
$1\frac{1}{2}$	cups asparagus in 2" lengths	$\frac{1}{4}$	teaspoon freshly ground pepper, or to taste
$\frac{1}{2}$	red bell pepper, coarsely chopped		
$\frac{1}{4}$	cup minced shallots		Freshly ground pepper and toasted pine nuts (see Tips, page 73) for garnish
$\frac{1}{2}$	cup Chardonnay or other rich, full-bodied white wine		

Bring a large pot of salted water to a boil over high heat. Cook the fettuccine according to the package directions.

Meanwhile, melt the butter with the oil in a large sauté pan over medium heat. Add the mushrooms, asparagus, bell pepper, and shallots. Cook, stirring occasionally, until the asparagus is tender, about 8 minutes. Reduce the heat to medium-low and add the wine. Use a wooden spoon to stir for about 3 minutes, scraping up the browned juices from the bottom of the pan. (The wine should not be evaporated.) Stir in the parsley and basil.

When the fettuccine is done, drain well. Add the noodles to the sauté pan and toss to combine with the mushroom mixture. Add the Parmesan and pepper and toss again. Taste and adjust the seasoning.

Garnish the servings with more pepper and pine nuts.

TIPS | ❧ *To store asparagus, treat it like cut flowers. Trim off the very ends of the stalks and place upright in water, or wrap the ends in wet paper towels in a plastic bag, then store the asparagus in the refrigerator for up to 1 week. If the stalks are thick, peel them for more even cooking and a tender stem.*

❧ *Flat-leaf, or Italian, parsley is preferable to the more common curly-leaf parsley for cooking because it boasts a brighter flavor and stands up to heat. Wash fresh parsley and shake off excess moisture, then wrap it in damp paper towels and store for up to 1 week in the refrigerator. Or, cut ½" off the stems and refrigerate, stem ends down, in a glass half-filled with water and covered with a plastic bag. Be sure to change the water every 2 days. Avoid using dried parsley, which has little of the distinctive parsley flavor.*

PENNE WITH TRIPLE-TOMATO PESTO

One of the joys of this pesto is that it can be made in advance and refrigerated in a covered container for up to 3 days. Reheat it and toss with freshly cooked pasta. The chèvre will melt into the dish, creating a luscious creamy topping. Kids may prefer a garnish of freshly grated Parmesan cheese.

MAKES 4 SERVINGS | VEGAN RECIPE (*if the goat cheese topping is omitted*)
WINE PAIRING: SANGIOVESE

For the pesto

¼	cup finely chopped, oil-packed sun-dried tomatoes (drain and set aside 1 tablespoon oil), see Tips		¼	cup Syrah or other full-bodied, peppery red wine
½	cup finely chopped onion		4	plum tomatoes, cut into ½" cubes
2	cloves garlic, minced		1	teaspoon sugar
1	can (15 ounces) diced tomatoes (see Tips)		¼	teaspoon salt, or to taste
			¼	teaspoon freshly ground pepper, or to taste

For the pasta

12	ounces (4 cups) penne		4	ounces fresh white goat cheese (chèvre), at room temperature
¼	cup finely chopped, fresh flat-leaf parsley			Freshly ground pepper and sprigs of fresh basil for garnish

To make the pesto, heat the reserved oil from the sun-dried tomatoes in a large, nonstick sauté pan over medium-high heat. Add the onion and cook, stirring occasionally, until translucent, about 5 minutes. Add the garlic and stir constantly for about 1 minute. Stir in the remaining pesto ingredients. Reduce the heat to medium and cook, uncovered, stirring occasionally until most of the liquid is evaporated, about 20 minutes.

To prepare the pasta, bring a large pot of salted water to a boil over high heat while the pesto is cooking. When the pesto has just 10 minutes remaining, cook the penne according to the package directions.

When the penne is done, drain well. Return it to the pot. Add the pesto and parsley and toss gently. Taste and adjust the seasoning.

Top each serving with a dollop of chèvre and garnish with pepper and basil sprigs.

TIPS | *❋ It takes about 17 pounds of fresh tomatoes to make 1 pound of dried tomatoes, so their intense flavor is a great way to add personality to tomato dishes.*

Oil-packed sun-dried tomatoes can be used directly from the jar. For most recipes, drain the oil, which can be used for cooking. Refrigerate open jars of oil-packed sun-dried tomatoes for up to 2 weeks.

Sun-dried tomatoes that are sold dry will keep indefinitely in a cool, dry place. Unless they are being used in a slow-cooked recipe that contains a significant amount of liquid, they must be rehydrated before using. Cover them with boiling water and soak for 15 to 30 minutes, or until they are soft and pliable. Drain before using; the flavored water can be used in some dishes.

❋ Good quality canned tomatoes are a better choice for cooked dishes than tomatoes that are fresh but underripe or out of season. Canned tomatoes are available diced or whole. Whole canned tomatoes can be cut right in the can by snipping them with kitchen shears.

Bow Ties
with Marsala-Mushroom Sauce

Polish the silver and light the candles! This elegant dish is perfect for company, and it's even more exceptional when prepared with a variety of mushrooms (see Tips), each offering its unique and robust flavor to the savory sauce.

MAKES 4 SERVINGS
WINE PAIRING: CHARDONNAY

8	ounces bow-tie pasta	¼	cup sweet Marsala wine
3	tablespoons olive oil, divided	2	teaspoons finely chopped fresh tarragon or ¼ teaspoon dried tarragon
4	cups sliced fresh mushrooms, such as cremini, shiitake, oyster, chanterelle, or a combination (about 12 ounces), see Tips	½	teaspoon salt, or to taste
¼	cup minced shallots	½	teaspoon freshly ground pepper, or to taste
3	cloves garlic, minced		Finely chopped fresh flat-leaf parsley for garnish
1	tablespoon all-purpose flour		
1	cup milk		

Bring a large pot of salted water to a boil over high heat. Cook the pasta according to the package directions.

Meanwhile, heat 2 tablespoons of the oil in a large sauté pan over medium heat. Add the mushrooms, shallots, and garlic. Cook, stirring occasionally, until tender, about 5 minutes.

Add the remaining 1 tablespoon of oil, then add the flour and stir until bubbly. Add the milk all at once and stir until thickened, about 3 minutes. Add the remaining ingredients, except the garnish, and stir until thoroughly warmed. Taste and adjust the seasoning.

When the pasta is done, drain well.

To serve, arrange the pasta in shallow pasta bowls, top with the sauce, and garnish with parsley.

TIPS | ❦ *Cremini mushrooms (sometimes labeled Italian brown mushrooms or baby bellas) have a denser, less watery texture and earthier, richer flavor than ordinary white mushrooms. Portobello mushrooms are cremini that have grown larger and matured.*

❦ *Fresh shiitake mushrooms are large, umbrella-shaped mushrooms, tan to brown-black in color, with an assertive, rich, uniquely woodsy flavor. Choose plump mushrooms with edges that turn under; avoid broken or shriveled caps. Store shiitake mushrooms in the refrigerator for up to 3 days, in a dish covered with a damp cloth or paper towel rather than in a closed container or plastic bag. The stems are very tough and should be removed. (They can be used to add flavor to stocks and sauces; discard the stems after they have been used for flavoring.)*

❦ *Oyster mushrooms are graceful, fluted mushrooms that vary in color from pale gray to dark brownish-gray. The seafoodlike flavor is robust and slightly peppery but becomes much milder when the mushrooms are cooked to a velvety texture. Look for firm, young mushrooms, $1^{1}/_{2}$" or less in diameter; remove the tough part of the stems before cooking.*

❦ *Chanterelles are trumpet-shaped wild mushrooms that range in color from bright yellow to orange. The flavor is nutty, and the texture is somewhat chewy. They are available fresh in some markets during the summer and winter months; dried chanterelles are available year-round and require hydrating before using in recipes.*

PENNE WITH RAINBOW PEPPERS AND RED ONION

A spectrum of beautiful bell peppers lends vibrant colors and sweetness to this pasta sauce. Add a dash of hot red-pepper flakes to give the sauce a piquant edge.

MAKES 4 SERVINGS | VEGAN RECIPE (*if cheese garnish is omitted*)
WINE PAIRING: RIESLING OR GEWÜRZTRAMINER

8	ounces penne	$\frac{1}{2}$	cup Merlot or other full-bodied, plummy red wine
3	tablespoons olive oil, divided	$\frac{1}{3}$	cup fresh basil chiffonade (see Tips, page 157)
1	red bell pepper, cut lengthwise into $\frac{1}{4}$"-wide strips (see Tips)	$\frac{1}{4}$	teaspoon salt, or to taste
1	yellow bell pepper, cut lengthwise into $\frac{1}{4}$"-wide strips	$\frac{1}{4}$	teaspoon freshly ground pepper, or to taste
1	orange bell pepper, cut lengthwise into $\frac{1}{4}$"-wide strips		Freshly ground pepper, freshly shredded Parmesan cheese, and toasted pine nuts (see Tips, page 73) for garnish
1	red onion, halved lengthwise, then thinly sliced		
4	cloves garlic, minced		
1	tomato, cut into $\frac{1}{2}$" cubes		

Bring a large pot of salted water to a boil over high heat. Cook the penne according to the package directions.

Heat 2 tablespoons of the oil in a large sauté pan over medium heat. Add the bell peppers and onion and cook, stirring occasionally, until tender, about 20 minutes. Add the garlic and stir constantly for about 1 minute. Stir in the tomato and wine, then reduce the heat to low and simmer until the liquid is nearly absorbed, about 10 minutes. Stir in the basil, salt, and pepper. Taste and adjust the seasoning.

When the pasta is done, drain well. Return it to the pan and toss with the remaining 1 tablespoon of oil.

To serve, spoon the bell pepper topping over the penne in shallow bowls. Garnish with pepper, Parmesan, and pine nuts.

TIPS | ✺ *Bell peppers are most often sold in the mature green stage, fully developed but not ripe. Red bell peppers are green peppers allowed to ripen on the vine; they are sweeter because of the longer ripening.*

Choose bell peppers that are plump, firm, and crisp, with no wrinkling or soft spots. Store them for up to 1 week in plastic bags in the refrigerator.

Spaghetti di Vino with Beets

My friend Judy Witts Francini offers cooking classes extraordinaire and market tours for my groups when I lead culinary travels to Florence, Italy. Her advice: "Everyone should try being Italian at least once a day." Take her words to heart and try this recipe I adapted from one of hers. It's simple and pretty—in a word, divine! Judy recommends using about 1 tablespoon butter in addition to the olive oil if your wine is tannic.

MAKES 4 SERVINGS | VEGAN RECIPE (*if cheese garnish is omitted*)
WINE PAIRING: PINOT GRIGIO

3	medium red or yellow beets, with 1" of stems still on (set aside greens), see Tips	¾	cup Merlot or other full-bodied, plummy red wine (with medium tannins)
8	ounces spaghetti	¼	cup dried currants
2	tablespoons olive oil	½	teaspoon salt, or to taste
1	large sweet onion, finely chopped (see Tips, page 71)	½	teaspoon freshly ground pepper, or to taste
2	cups finely sliced reserved beet greens	2	tablespoons fresh lemon juice
4	cloves garlic, minced	¼	cup toasted pine nuts (see Tips, page 73)
			Freshly ground pepper and crumbled feta cheese for garnish

Bring a medium saucepan of salted water to a boil over high heat. Add the beets and reduce the heat to medium-low. Cover and simmer until the beets can be pierced with a knife, about 30 to 45 minutes. (Or, place the beets in a microwaveable dish with about ¼ cup salted water and cover with a lid or plastic wrap. Microwave on high power for 8 minutes, or until thoroughly cooked, turning the beets at 2-minute intervals.)

When the beets are cool enough to handle, remove the skins (see Tips). Cut the beets into 2" × ¼" strips.

Bring a large pot of salted water to a boil. Cook the spaghetti 2 to 3 minutes less than the package directions suggest. (The pasta should be slightly undercooked but not crunchy.)

While the pasta is cooking, heat the oil in a large sauté pan over medium heat. Add the onion and cook, stirring occasionally, until translucent, about 5 minutes. Add the beet greens and garlic and stir constantly until the greens are wilted, about 1 minute.

Stir in the beets, wine, dried currants, salt, and pepper. Cook, stirring often, for about 5 minutes. The wine should be reduced but not totally evaporated. Stir in the lemon juice.

When the pasta is cooked according to the above instructions, drain it well. Return it to the pot and add the beet mixture. Stir over medium heat until the spaghetti absorbs the wine and turns red. Remove from the heat. Add the pine nuts and toss again. Taste and adjust the seasoning. (Remember that the feta cheese garnish will add saltiness.)

Garnish the servings with pepper and feta cheese.

TIPS | ❧ *Choose firm, evenly shaped, smooth-skinned, small to medium beets; oversized ones may be woody. It's best if the greens are attached; they should be bright green with no signs of wilting. As soon as you bring the beets home, cut off the tops, leaving about 1" of the stem attached to the beet. Refrigerate the beets, unwashed, in a plastic bag for up to 2 weeks. The greens will keep, unwashed, in a separate plastic bag for up to 3 days.*

To prepare the beets for cooking, leave 1" of the stems and the root ends intact. Scrub well, taking care not to break the skin—beets lose color and nutrients if the skin breaks. After cooking, let the beets cool enough to handle, and then rub off the skins under running water or remove them with a paring knife. To avoid staining your hands, wear disposable plastic gloves; also protect the cutting board with plastic wrap or waxed paper.

Pasta Primavera

This ode to spring is simple—and simply sublime. The light pasta dish calls for the freshest, top-quality ingredients both combined and paired with high-acid white wine.

MAKES 4 SERVINGS | VEGAN RECIPE (*if cheese garnish is omitted*)
WINE PAIRING: PINOT BLANC

12	ounces bow-tie or other short pasta of your choice	2	tablespoons fresh lemon juice
4	tablespoons extra-virgin olive oil, divided	2	tablespoons fresh basil chiffonade (see Tips)
1	carrot, julienned (see Tips)	1	tablespoon snipped fresh dill
1½	cups green beans or asparagus spears in 2" lengths	¼	teaspoon salt, or to taste
1	small yellow summer squash, julienned	¼	teaspoon freshly ground pepper, or to taste
1	small zucchini, julienned	⅛	teaspoon red-pepper flakes, or to taste
2	leeks, white parts only, halved lengthwise and cut into ¼"-wide strips (see Tips, page 61)		Freshly ground pepper, freshly grated Romano cheese, and toasted pine nuts (see Tips, page 73) for garnish
½	red bell pepper, finely chopped		
⅓	cup Sauvignon Blanc or other medium-bodied, high-acid white wine		

Bring a large pot of salted water to a boil over high heat. Cook the pasta according to the package directions.

Meanwhile, heat 2 tablespoons of the oil in a large sauté pan over medium-high heat. Add the carrot and green beans or asparagus and cook, stirring occasionally, until the vegetables are nearly tender, about 8 minutes. Add the summer squash, zucchini, leeks, and bell pepper. Continue cooking, stirring occasionally, until all the vegetables are tender, about 4 more minutes.

In a measuring cup, stir together the remaining ingredients, except the garnish. Pour into the sauté pan and stir until the wine is nearly evaporated. Taste and adjust the seasoning.

When the pasta is done, drain it well. Return it to the pan, add the remaining 2 tablespoons of oil, and toss.

Transfer servings of pasta to individual bowls. Top with the vegetable mixture and garnish with pepper, Romano, and pine nuts.

TIPS | ❧ *To* julienne *is to cut foods into matchstick strips about ¹/₈" thick.*

❧ *Vegetable leaves, such as lettuce and spinach, and large-leafed herbs, such as basil, can be cut into shreds—sometimes called a* **chiffonade**, *which comes from a French word that describes something that has been torn into ribbons or shreds. To make chiffonade cuts, stack several leaves on a cutting board, roll them up lengthwise, and then slice crosswise into thin strips.*

Zucchini Stuffed with Lentils and Tomatoes

This hearty dish can lie in waiting for a hungry family on a busy night, for once the vegetables are chopped, most of the preparation work is over. For a showier presentation, serve the zucchini on beds of warm wilted spinach seasoned with fresh lemon juice, salt, and pepper.

MAKES 6 SERVINGS | VEGAN RECIPE (*if cheese garnish is omitted*)
WINE PAIRING: PINOT NOIR OR CÔTES DU RHÔNE

⅓	cup brown lentils	¼	cup tomato paste
½	cup Pinot Noir or other medium-bodied, earthy red wine	¼	cup finely chopped walnuts
½	cup water	2	tablespoons finely chopped fresh flat-leaf parsley
1	large carrot, finely chopped	2	teaspoons finely chopped fresh thyme or ½ teaspoon dried thyme
1	rib celery, finely chopped		
½	cup finely chopped onion	1	teaspoon snipped fresh dill or ¼ teaspoon dried dillweed (see Tips)
¼	green bell pepper, finely chopped		
2	cloves garlic, minced	1	teaspoon finely chopped fresh tarragon or ¼ teaspoon dried tarragon
1	bay leaf		
6	medium (1½"-diameter) zucchini	¼	cup freshly grated Parmesan cheese
	Dash + ¼ teaspoon salt, or to taste	¼	cup dried bread crumbs
	Dash + ¼ teaspoon freshly ground pepper		

Combine the lentils, wine, water, carrot, celery, onion, bell pepper, garlic, and bay leaf in a large saucepan. Cover and simmer over medium-high heat until the lentils are tender and the liquid is absorbed, about 30 minutes.

Meanwhile, preheat the oven to 350°F. Lightly oil a 10" × 8" baking dish. Bring a large pot of water to a boil over high heat, add the zucchini, and cook until just tender, about 15 minutes. Drain and cool slightly.

Trim the ends and slice each zucchini in half lengthwise. Use a spoon to scoop out about half of the inside of the zucchini (and discard), leaving a ¼"-thick shell. Arrange the zucchini shells in the prepared pan and sprinkle with a dash of salt and freshly ground pepper.

When the lentils are cooked, remove the bay leaf. Stir in the remaining ¼ teaspoon salt and pepper, tomato paste, walnuts, parsley, thyme, dill, and tarragon. Taste and adjust the seasoning.

Stir together the Parmesan, bread crumbs, and a dash of pepper in a small bowl.

Spread about 2 tablespoons of the lentil mixture into each zucchini half. Sprinkle with the Parmesan mixture.

Bake for 30 minutes, or until the zucchini are completely tender and the cheese is melted.

TIPS | ❧ *Dill is a sharply aromatic herb with a lemony taste. When using fresh dill, cut the feathery dill tips with scissors. Dried dillweed is acceptable, but it is stronger than fresh, so use it in moderation.*

CARROT PATTIES
WITH ORANGE-SHERRY SAUCE

Drizzled with a sherry sauce, piquant with a hint of jalapeños, and sweetened with a touch of orange, a trio of these patties makes a hearty main course. You can also serve one patty solo as a first course or arrange a plateful on your appetizer buffet.

MAKES 4 SERVINGS (*3 patties per serving*)
WINE PAIRING: PINOT BLANC

For the sauce

¼	cup mayonnaise
¼	cup fresh orange juice
2	tablespoons dry sherry
1	tablespoon extra-virgin olive oil

2	teaspoons minced fresh jalapeño pepper, or to taste (wear plastic gloves when handling)
1	teaspoon sugar
⅛	teaspoon salt, or to taste

For the patties

¼	cup olive oil, divided
2	cups coarsely shredded carrots (about 4 carrots)
1	cup finely chopped red onion (see Tips)
1	rib celery, finely chopped
4	cloves garlic, minced
1	cup dried bread crumbs

½	cup slivered almonds, finely crushed or ground
¼	cup coarsely chopped fresh flat-leaf parsley
2	eggs, lightly beaten
¼	teaspoon salt
	Thin avocado slices and sprigs of fresh flat-leaf parsley for garnish

To make the sauce, whisk together all the ingredients in a small saucepan until smooth. Set aside.

To make the patties, heat 2 tablespoons of the oil in a large skillet over medium-high heat. Add the carrots, onion, and celery. Cook, stirring occasionally, until tender, about 8 minutes. Add the garlic and stir constantly for about 1 minute. Remove from the heat and stir in the remaining ingredients, except the garnishes. Let cool.

For each patty, gently squeeze about ¼ cup of the mixture in your hand to form a ball and then flatten into a 3" round, about ⅜" thick. Place the patties on a plate as they are prepared. Wash the skillet.

Heat the remaining 2 tablespoons of oil in the skillet over medium heat. Cook the patties for about 5 minutes on each side, or until lightly browned.

To serve, arrange 3 patties on each plate. Drizzle with the sauce and garnish with the avocado slices and parsley sprigs.

TIPS | ❧ *Red or purple onions (sometimes called Bermuda onions, though not from Bermuda) will keep for 2 to 4 weeks when stored in a cool, dry, dark place with good air circulation. After cooking, they retain a sweeter flavor than white onions.*

VEGETARIAN CASSOULET

This rustic dish from the Languedoc region of France traditionally is made with white beans and a variety of robust meats, including sausage and whatever the hunter of the family has brought to the kitchen. Legend has it that cassoulet came to being during the Hundred Years' War, when the town's cooks threw together beans and meat to propel their troops into battle. Here, it's made with canned beans and vegetarian soy sausage, available in health food stores and in the freezer section of many supermarkets. And, spared the lengthy cooking that meat requires, this dish is quick to prepare.

MAKES 4 SERVINGS | VEGAN RECIPE (*if meatless sausage is vegan*)
WINE PAIRING: CABERNET SAUVIGNON

4	sprigs fresh flat-leaf parsley	½	cup Cabernet Sauvignon or other full-bodied red wine
2	sprigs fresh thyme		
1	bay leaf	¼	teaspoon salt, or to taste
4	tablespoons olive oil, divided	¼	teaspoon freshly ground pepper, or to taste
1	large onion, coarsely chopped		
2	carrots, coarsely chopped	¼	teaspoon red-pepper flakes
1	rib celery, coarsely chopped	1	package (10 ounces) meatless frozen sausage (4 sausages)
4	cloves garlic, minced		
1	can (15 ounces) great Northern beans, drained and rinsed	½	cup dried bread crumbs
			Sprigs of fresh flat-leaf parsley for garnish
1	can (15 ounces) diced tomatoes		

Preheat the oven to 400°F. Lightly oil a 2½-quart baking dish.

Wrap the parsley, thyme, and bay leaf in a cheesecloth bag and tie it with kitchen twine (see Tips). Set aside.

Heat 2 tablespoons of the oil in a Dutch oven over medium heat. Add the onion, carrots, and celery. Cook, stirring occasionally, until tender, about 10 minutes.

Add the garlic and stir constantly for about 1 minute. Stir in the beans, tomatoes (with juice), wine, salt, pepper, red-pepper flakes, and the bag of herbs. Reduce the heat to medium-low, cover, and cook for 20 minutes.

Meanwhile, pour ½ cup water into a medium skillet over medium heat. Cook the frozen sausages, covered, for about 10 minutes, then drain and cut the sausages into 1" chunks. Add 1 tablespoon of oil to the pan and cook the sausages, turning them occasionally, until all sides are lightly browned, about 5 minutes.

Remove the bag of herbs from the beans and discard it. Transfer ½ cup of the bean mixture to a blender (or food processor) and purée until smooth, then stir the purée into the remaining beans. Stir in the sausage. Taste and adjust the seasoning, then pour the mixture into the prepared baking dish.

Combine the bread crumbs with the remaining 1 tablespoon of oil in a small bowl. Spread over the top of the beans.

Bake the cassoulet in the preheated oven for 20 minutes, or until it is thoroughly heated and the bread crumb topping is lightly browned.

Garnish the servings with parsley sprigs.

TIPS | ❧ *A bouquet garni is a bundle of assorted fresh or dried herbs either placed in a double-layer cheesecloth bag, enclosed in a tea infuser, or tied together with kitchen twine. Lightly bruising the herbs first with a small mallet or pestle helps to release their aromas and flavors into soups, stews, broths, and other slow-cooking dishes. Leave a long end of string to tie to the pot handle for easy removal, or remove the herb bundle with a fork or slotted spoon at the end of the cooking time.*

Vegetable Frittata

Frittatas are to Italians what omelettes are to the French. While the ingredients may be the same, the difference lies in the cooking method. In a frittata, the filling is mixed right with the eggs, then the mixture is cooked together and left open-faced. True to its Italian nature, the recipe is very flexible; you may add or substitute other vegetables (up to 3 cups total), such as sliced zucchini or tomatoes. Prepare the Roasted Red Bell Pepper Sauce (page 170) or Sangiovese Tomato Sauce (page 166) in advance, and reheat in a small saucepan while the frittata cooks.

MAKES 6 SERVINGS
WINE PAIRING: BEAUJOLAIS OR CÔTES DU RHÔNE

2	tablespoons unsalted butter	2	tablespoons finely chopped fresh basil or $^1/_2$ teaspoon dried basil
2	small red potatoes, very thinly sliced (see Tips)	1	teaspoon finely chopped fresh oregano or $^1/_4$ teaspoon dried oregano
1	cup sliced mushrooms (about 3 ounces)		
$^1/_2$	red or green bell pepper, cut into 2" × $^1/_4$" strips	$^1/_4$	teaspoon salt
$^1/_4$	cup thinly sliced onion	$^1/_4$	teaspoon freshly ground pepper
2	cloves garlic, minced	$^1/_2$	cup Roasted Red Bell Pepper Sauce (*page 170*) or Sangiovese Tomato Sauce (*page 166*)
4	eggs, lightly beaten (see Tips)		
2	tablespoons water		Freshly ground pepper, freshly grated Parmesan cheese, and sprigs of fresh basil for garnish
$^1/_4$	cup freshly grated Parmesan cheese		

Position the oven broiler rack about 5" from the heating element. Preheat the broiler.

Melt the butter in a large, ovenproof skillet over medium heat. Add the potatoes and cook, turning occasionally, until almost tender and not browned, about 5 minutes. Add the mushrooms, bell pepper, and onion. Cook, stirring occasionally, until the vegetables are tender, about 4 more minutes. Add the garlic and stir constantly for about 1 minute.

Meanwhile, lightly beat the eggs and water with a fork or whisk just long enough to combine. Whisk in the Parmesan, basil, oregano, salt, and pepper. Pour the mixture over the cooked vegetables in the skillet and tilt to distribute the eggs evenly. Reduce the heat to medium-low and cook, undisturbed, until the eggs are set on the bottom but the top is still runny, 3 to 5 minutes. Place under the broiler for about 2 minutes, or until the top is set and lightly browned.

Serve the frittata directly from the skillet or loosen it around the edges with a spatula and slide the frittata onto a serving platter. Cut it into wedges and drizzle each serving with a heaping tablespoon of the sauce. Garnish with pepper, Parmesan, and basil sprigs.

TIPS | ❦ *Red potatoes are thin-skinned and sweet. They are also low in starch, which prevents them from breaking apart easily after cooking. Do not refrigerate before cooking; store them for up to 2 weeks at room temperature in a cool, dark place.*

❦ *Store uncooked eggs in their carton, large ends up, in the coldest part of your refrigerator (not in the refrigerator door) for up to 1 month. They will keep for 4 weeks beyond the carton date, but for the best flavor, use them within 1 week. To tell whether an egg is fresh, place it in a bowl of salted, cool water. If it sinks, it's fresh; if it floats, discard it.*

Sangiovese Tomato Sauce

I've come to count on this aromatic sauce as an (almost) all-purpose tomato–red wine sauce. I love it generously spooned over Polenta Triangles (page 120) and Roasted Vegetables (page 123), drizzled over Lasagna Rolls (page 144), used as a topping for the Vegetable Frittata (page 164), or simply tossed with pasta. It will keep for up to 2 days in a covered container in the refrigerator. Another bonus: The recipe multiplies easily.

MAKES 1 CUP | VEGAN RECIPE

1	tablespoon olive oil	1	tablespoon finely chopped fresh basil
1	shallot, minced	1	tablespoon finely chopped fresh flat-leaf parsley
1	clove garlic, minced		
1	pound (about 6) plum tomatoes, peeled and quartered (see Tips)	⅛	teaspoon red-pepper flakes, or to taste
¼	cup Sangiovese or other medium-bodied, high-acid red wine	¼	teaspoon salt, or to taste
½	teaspoon sugar		Dash of freshly ground pepper, or to taste

Heat the oil in a medium saucepan over medium heat. Add the shallot and garlic and cook, stirring constantly, until tender, about 2 minutes. Stir in the tomatoes, wine, and sugar. When the liquid begins to bubble, reduce the heat to medium-low. Cover and cook until the tomatoes are completely softened, about 15 minutes.

Let the sauce cool for a few minutes, then transfer it to a blender and purée. Stir the purée through a mesh strainer to remove the seeds. Return the sauce to the saucepan, then stir in the basil, parsley, red-pepper flakes, salt, and pepper. Taste and adjust the seasoning.

TIPS | ❧ *Plum, or Roma, tomatoes have thick, meaty walls, small seeds, little juice, and a rich, sweet flavor. Because they're less juicy, they are the best choice for recipes that benefit from tomatoes that retain their shape after being chopped or sliced. Store them in a cool but not cold spot—never in the refrigerator.*

❧ *To peel a tomato, first core it with a paring knife, removing the stem end and white center. Cut an "x" on the bottom, carefully piercing just through the skin. Then immerse the tomato in a pot of boiling water just long enough to loosen the skin without cooking the tomato (5 seconds for a very ripe tomato, 10 to 20 seconds for a firmer tomato). Remove with a slotted spoon and immediately plunge into a bowl of very cold water. Let it stand for about 1 minute. When the tomato is cool enough to handle, use a paring knife to slip off the skin, which will have become very loose.*

Spicy Merlot Marinara

This wine-scented sauce is delicious poured over an omelette or pasta. I especially enjoy combining it with fettuccine (about 2 ounces dried pasta per serving) and Ruby Port–Glazed Portobello Mushrooms (page 124). If you prefer a less spicy sauce, simply reduce or omit the red-pepper flakes.

Makes 2½ cups | Vegan recipe

2	tablespoons olive oil	2	teaspoons finely chopped fresh oregano or ½ teaspoon dried oregano
½	cup finely chopped onion		
1	carrot, finely chopped	2	teaspoons finely chopped fresh thyme or ½ teaspoon dried thyme
½	green bell pepper, finely chopped		
2	cloves garlic, minced	½	teaspoon packed brown sugar
1	can (15 ounces) diced tomatoes	¼	teaspoon salt, or to taste
2	tablespoons tomato paste	¼	teaspoon freshly ground pepper, or to taste
½	cup Merlot or other full-bodied, plummy red wine	⅛	teaspoon red-pepper flakes, or to taste
¼	cup water		
1	tablespoon finely chopped fresh basil or ½ teaspoon dried basil (see Tips)		Sprigs of fresh basil, oregano, or thyme for garnish

Heat the oil in a large saucepan over medium heat. Add the onion, carrot, and bell pepper and cook until the carrot is almost tender, about 5 minutes. Add the garlic and stir constantly for about 1 minute. Stir in the remaining ingredients, except the fresh basil (if using). When the mixture comes to a simmer, reduce the heat to low. Cover and cook, stirring occasionally, for 10 minutes.

Uncover and continue to cook, stirring occasionally until the sauce thickens and is reduced to 2½ cups, about 8 to 10 minutes. (If you prefer a thinner sauce, reduce the cooking time accordingly.) Add the fresh basil (if using) during the last 5 minutes. Taste and adjust the seasoning. Garnish each serving with a fresh herb sprig.

TIPS | *❧ Fresh herbs, which come from the leafy parts of plants, contain more moisture and therefore are milder than dried herbs. When substituting, use about 3 to 4 times more fresh herbs than dried herbs.*

❧ Dried herbs will remain flavorful for about 1 year when stored in a tightly closed container (rather than in a box) in a dark, dry place. It's a good idea to date the jars when you buy them. The herbs should resemble the color they were when fresh and should not be dull or brownish green. To get the most out of dried herbs, crumble them between your fingers to release the aromatics as you add them to recipes.

ROASTED RED BELL PEPPER SAUCE

This lovely, velvety sauce has long been one of my favorites. It graces every dish it tops—spooned over Lasagna Rolls (page 144), Vegetable Frittata (page 164), or Ruby Port–Glazed Portobello Mushrooms (page 124). Since the roasted red bell peppers in a jar work just fine, you'll discover it's also a simple way to add the aroma and flavor of red wine to other dishes already in your repertoire.

MAKES ABOUT ¾ CUP | VEGAN RECIPE

1   cup drained and coarsely chopped, store-bought roasted red bell peppers, or 2 freshly roasted red bell peppers, coarsely chopped (see Tips)

1   tablespoon extra-virgin olive oil

2   cloves garlic, minced

1   teaspoon sugar

¼   teaspoon freshly ground pepper, or to taste

¼   teaspoon salt, or to taste

⅛   teaspoon red-pepper flakes, or to taste

¼   cup Shiraz or other full-bodied, ripe-jammy red wine

Process all the sauce ingredients, except the wine, in a blender or food processor until smooth. Transfer the mixture to a small saucepan. Stir in the wine. Simmer, covered, over medium heat, stirring occasionally for 5 minutes. Taste and adjust the seasoning.

TIPS | ❦ *To roast bell peppers, preheat the broiler and line a baking sheet with aluminum foil. Remove and discard the stems. Then cut each bell pepper in half lengthwise and remove and discard the seeds and ribs. Place the pepper halves, skin side up, in a single layer on the prepared pan; flatten each with the palm of your hand. Lightly brush the skins with olive oil. Broil for about 15 minutes, or until the halves are fork-tender and the skins are blackened and blistered. Transfer the pepper halves to a heavy-duty zip-top bag or brown paper bag and seal. Set aside until cool for about 20 minutes. (The steam will loosen the skins.) Remove the halves from the bag. Peel the peppers with your hands, using a paring knife to scrape away any peel that doesn't come off easily. Discard the skins.*

Whole bell peppers also can be roasted on a grill over a hot charcoal fire, or over the flame of a gas stove. Remove the stem and seeds before using. Use right away, or store the peeled peppers and their juices in a covered container in the refrigerator for up to 1 week.

DESSERTS

FOR MANY OF US, dessert is an anticipated and irresistible part of the meal. Now you can create a whole new collection of extra-ordinary, enticing desserts that offer the sensual qualities of sweet wines and liqueurs. In many desserts, the aroma and flavor, as well as the alcoholic nature, are prominent, so it's important to use good-quality spirits and to add them with discretion.

Making a luxurious dessert can be as simple as spiking fruit with spirits. Gourmet shops sell "cooks' shots," a syringe-type kitchen tool that allows you to inject liquor into fruit, such as Cointreau into strawberries, Kahlúa into oranges, or gin into watermelon. Or, you can cut a small hole through the rind of a watermelon, pour rum into the opening, reinsert the plug, and refrigerate the melon overnight while the fruit becomes high-spirited. You can soak sliced fresh fruits, such as peaches, in port or sweet Madeira for an hour or so to make a lively topping for frozen yogurt or ice cream.

Here you'll find satisfying desserts that are especially tempting when served warm, including Chocolate-Cherry Bread Pudding with Sherry Cream (*page 176*), Pear and Almond Tart (*page 178*), and Broiled Bananas with Rum-Raisin Sauce (*page 196*). Many of these free-spirited finales, such as Triple Chocolate–Cassis Brownies (*page 180*) and Apricot Brandy Pound Cake (*page 182*), can be made in advance and savored later at room temperature. Macerated fruit, too, becomes zestier after time to rest. Later, it's invigorating when served chilled at the end of a meal or as a spirited snack.

Other desserts, including silky-smooth-textured Strawberry-Shiraz Sorbet (*page 208*) and icy Citrus-Mint Granitas (*page 210*), are frozen. Both alcohol and sugar lower the freezing point of water, so mixtures containing liquor take longer to set up.

In addition to using store-bought liquor, I've provided recipes for Limoncello (*page 188*) and Coffee-Flavored Liqueur (*page 191*). Not only are they fun to make, but these sublime brews also make elegant gifts. Among your friends, you just may become known for serving spectacular sundaes topped with divinely hedonistic, liqueur-laced Hot Fudge Sauce (*page 212*) and crimson Raspberry-Merlot Sauce (*page 213*). And they'll be in ecstasy over Watermelon Poptails (*page 209*), which offer a tantalizing way to cool off on a steamy day.

These *spirited vegetarian* desserts deserve voluptuous presentation. Use elegant or splashy dishes, and remember garnishes, such as edible flowers—they'll add style to the plates.

If you choose to serve spirits with your desserts, select sweet dessert wines and fortified wines for the perfect flirtatious finale. ❧

APPLE-CHERRY CRISP

My friend Leslie Levich Knight and I shared classes and school lunches from kindergarten through college. Now we share recipes, travel tips, and gourmet meals. Leslie is known among friends for this autumn dessert. She recommends using a variety of apples, such as Granny Smith, McIntosh, and Braeburn, each of which offers its own unique flavor and texture.

MAKES ONE 9" × 9" BAKING DISH (*6 servings*)

1	cup (5 ounces) dried cherries	$\frac{1}{2}$	cup sugar
$\frac{1}{3}$	cup apple brandy, such as Calvados or applejack	$\frac{1}{2}$	teaspoon ground cinnamon
1	cup all-purpose flour (see Tips)	$\frac{1}{2}$	teaspoon salt
$\frac{1}{2}$	cup (1 stick) unsalted butter, cut into about 6 pieces	4	large apples, cored, peeled, and cut into $\frac{3}{8}$"-thick wedges (6 to 7 cups)

Combine the dried cherries and apple brandy in a small bowl. Cover and let stand at room temperature for at least 2 or up to 8 hours.

Preheat the oven to 350°F. Lightly coat a 9" × 9" baking dish with cooking spray.

Combine the flour, butter, sugar, cinnamon, and salt in a food processor. Pulse until the mixture looks like oatmeal. (Or combine the ingredients with your hands or with a pastry blender.)

Put the sliced apples in a large bowl, add the cherry-brandy mixture, and toss. Spread in the bottom of the prepared baking dish. Cover evenly with the flour mixture.

Bake for 35 to 40 minutes, or until the top is lightly browned, the liquid is bubbly, and the apples are fork-tender.

TIPS | *❧ Transfer flour from the bag to an airtight container and store at room temperature for up to 6 months. If the temperature is above 75°F, store it in the refrigerator or freezer.*

CHOCOLATE-CHERRY BREAD PUDDING WITH SHERRY CREAM

This lusty dessert not only wins applause, but it also transforms day-old bread into a gourmet comfort food. I like it best served warm; if you make it in advance, you can reheat individual servings in the microwave oven. The sherry cream makes a heavenly topping, but sometimes I top the bread pudding with scoops of pistachio ice cream instead. To serve with a spirit, pour Tawny Port, which is always luscious with chocolate.

MAKES ONE 9" × 9" BAKING DISH (*8 servings*)

For the bread pudding

½	cup dried cherries	1	teaspoon pure vanilla extract
¼	cup Cognac or other brandy	¼	teaspoon ground cinnamon
8	ounces semisweet chocolate, coarsely chopped	1½	cups day-old whole wheat bread in ½" cubes (about 2 slices)
4	eggs	½	cup sliced toasted almonds (see Tips, page 73)
½	cup sugar		
1	cup half-and-half		

For the sherry cream

½	cup heavy cream	1	tablespoon sweet (cream) sherry
2	teaspoons sugar		Sweetened cocoa powder for garnish

To make the bread pudding, combine the dried cherries and Cognac in a small bowl. Cover and let stand at room temperature for at least 2 or up to 8 hours.

Melt the chocolate in the top of a double boiler over simmering water (see Tips, page 212). Stir until smooth. Remove the pan from the double boiler and let cool to room temperature, about 10 minutes. (Or, put the chocolate in a microwaveable dish and melt in the microwave oven on medium power for about 4 to 6 minutes, stirring halfway through.)

In a large bowl, beat the eggs and sugar together until light. Whisk in the cooled chocolate, the half-and-half, vanilla, and cinnamon until the mixture is smooth. Stir in the cherries and Cognac, bread cubes, and almonds.

Pour the mixture into the prepared baking dish and let stand for 30 minutes, or cover and refrigerate for up to 2 hours.

Preheat the oven to 325°F. Lightly coat a 9" × 9" baking dish with cooking spray.

Bake for 40 minutes, or until set in the middle. The pudding will pull away slightly from the edges of the dish.

To make the sherry cream, just before serving, beat the cream with the sugar in a chilled small bowl until soft peaks form (see Tips, page 201). Gently fold in the sherry.

Serve the bread pudding warm or at room temperature. Cover and refrigerate for up to 3 days.

Top bowls of the bread pudding with the flavored whipped cream and lightly dust with cocoa powder stirred through a fine-mesh strainer.

PEAR AND ALMOND TART

This elegant dessert, adapted from the recipe my friend Tom Nugent claims as his favorite, takes just minutes to prepare and then bakes on its own, filling your kitchen with an enticing aroma. To serve the tart warm, pop it into the oven just as you and your guests sit down for dinner. Muscat or Sauterne makes a lovely pairing, should you wish to serve wine with dessert.

For variety, substitute hazelnut-flavored liqueur (such as Frangelico) for the almond-flavored liqueur, and hazelnuts (skins removed) for the almonds.

MAKES ONE 9" TART (*8 servings*)

For the cookie crust

3	tablespoons unsalted butter	1	egg yolk (see Tips)
¼	cup sugar	¾	cup all-purpose flour

For the filling

¾	cup heavy cream	¼	teaspoon ground cinnamon (see Tips)
¼	cup sugar		
¼	cup all-purpose flour	2	fresh pears (ripe but not soft), peeled, cored, and halved, each half cut into about six ½"-thick wedges
¼	cup almond-flavored liqueur, such as Amaretto di Saronno		
¼	teaspoon salt	¼	cup sliced almonds

Preheat the oven to 400°F.

To make the crust, use an electric mixer to cream the butter in a small bowl. Add the sugar and egg yolk and beat until smooth. Using a fork, stir in the flour until it is well-blended and forms fine crumbs. (Or prepare the crust in a food processor, using a pulsing motion.) Press the mixture into the bottom and up the sides of a 9" pie plate. Bake until slightly firm, about 10 minutes. (The crust will be slightly firm but not browned.) Set aside to cool.

Meanwhile, to prepare the filling, whisk together the cream, sugar, flour, liqueur, salt, and cinnamon in a medium bowl until smooth.

Arrange the pears, pinwheel style (thickest portions to the outside edge), on the prepared crust. Save 2 pear wedges, cut them in half horizontally, and arrange in the center. Pour the cream mixture evenly over the pears. Sprinkle with the almonds.

Place the pie plate on a baking sheet and bake for about 25 minutes, or until the top is lightly browned and the sauce is not runny. (It will be like custard, and not firm.) Let stand for at least 15 minutes before slicing. Serve warm or at room temperature.

TIPS | *❧ To separate egg whites from yolks, separate one egg at a time into a cup or small bowl. The most basic method is to use your hand: Cup your hand and crack the egg into it; the white slips through your fingers while the yolk stays in your palm. Or you can use an egg separator or funnel. It's not a good idea to separate eggs by passing the yolk back and forth from one half of a shell to the other because bacteria on the shell's surface may be transferred to the egg.*

❧ Cinnamon is the inner bark of a tropical evergreen tree. When dried, it curls into long quills, which are cut into shorter lengths and sold as cinnamon sticks or ground into powder. When stored, the sticks retain the distinctive flavor longer than the powder.

Triple Chocolate–Cassis Brownies

Love at first bite: The moment I first sampled this decadent dessert at a friend's house, I was smitten. Lis Viehweg, who shared her fabulous recipe, recommends serving these dense, fudge-like brownies in small pieces. She suggests creating variations on the theme by substituting other fruit-flavored liqueurs, such as raspberry. I find that Ruby Port also adds a nice touch. For a dessert pairing, pour small glasses of raspberry-flavored liqueur, such as framboise.

Makes one 13" × 9" pan (*30 brownies*)

6	ounces bittersweet chocolate, coarsely chopped (see Tips)	3	eggs
		1	cup sugar
6	ounces semisweet chocolate, coarsely chopped	¾	cup packed brown sugar
		½	cup crème de cassis liqueur
2	ounces unsweetened chocolate, coarsely chopped	2	teaspoons pure vanilla extract
1	cup butter	1¼	cups all-purpose flour
¼	cup unsweetened cocoa powder	¼	teaspoon salt

Preheat the oven to 350°F. Lightly coat a 13" × 9" baking pan with cooking spray.

Combine the chocolates with the butter and cocoa powder in the top pan of a double boiler, over barely simmering water (see Tips, page 212). Stir as the chocolates melt, until smooth. Remove the top portion of the double boiler and let it stand until the mixture is lukewarm, about 10 minutes.

Meanwhile, lightly beat the eggs in a large bowl. Add the sugars and beat with an electric mixer at high speed until thick and light-colored, about 5 minutes. Beat in the crème de cassis and vanilla. Add the chocolate mixture and beat until well-blended. With the mixer on low speed, gradually add the flour and salt. Beat just until combined.

Pour the batter into the prepared pan and smooth the surface with a rubber spatula. Bake for about 30 minutes, or until a toothpick inserted 2" from the center comes out slightly moist.

Cool the brownies in the pan on a rack. When completely cool, cut the brownies into 30 squares. (Use a sharp knife and dip it in cool water for clean cuts.) Refrigerate the brownies with waxed paper between layers in a covered pan.

TIPS | ❧ *Chocolate should be stored, tightly wrapped, in a cool (60° to 70°F), dry place, where it will keep for years. Because it scorches easily, melt it in a double boiler over barely simmering water, or in a microwave oven on medium power.*

APRICOT BRANDY POUND CAKE

This cake has been among the favorites in my repertoire for decades. Serve one cake fresh from the oven; freeze the other to have on hand for unexpected guests. Top slices of the cake with dollops of sweetened whipped cream and Brandied Fruit (opposite page).

MAKES TWO 9" × 5" LOAF PANS (*about 8 servings each*)

2	sticks (8 ounces) unsalted butter, softened	½	teaspoon salt
		¼	teaspoon baking soda (see Tips)
2	cups sugar	1	cup sour cream
6	eggs	½	cup apricot brandy
1½	cups all-purpose flour	1	teaspoon pure vanilla extract
1½	cups whole-wheat flour		

Preheat the oven to 325°F. Lightly grease and flour two 9" × 5" loaf pans.

Use an electric mixer to cream the butter in a medium bowl. Add about half the sugar and beat until it is well-blended, and then add the remaining sugar. Beat until the mixture is fluffy, scraping down the sides of the mixing bowl as needed. Beat in the eggs, one at a time.

Combine the flours, salt, and baking soda in a medium bowl.

Stir together the remaining ingredients in a small bowl.

Alternately add the flour and sour cream mixtures to the butter mixture, stirring until just blended.

Pour the batter into the prepared pans. Bake for about 1¼ hours, or until a toothpick inserted into the centers comes out clean. Cool in the pan on a rack for about 10 minutes. Run a knife between the edges of the cakes and the pans and then remove the cakes from the pans. Turn right side up and cool completely on the rack.

To store the cakes, after they are completely cool, wrap them in plastic and refrigerate. Add a layer of foil if freezing. Or, cut the cake into individual slices: Place the slices in zip-top bags, press to remove the excess air from the bags, seal, and freeze for up to 4 months.

TIPS | ✿ *Store baking soda in a cool, dry place for up to 6 months, or longer if you use an airtight container. To test for freshness, stir ¼ teaspoon baking soda into 2 teaspoons vinegar; bubbles indicate that the baking soda is still active.*

BRANDIED FRUIT

This is a very forgiving as well as scrumptious recipe, for you can vary the fruits to use your favorites at the peak of the season. Serve the medley over Apricot Brandy Pound Cake (opposite page), on ice cream, or as a light dessert on its own.

MAKES 6 SERVINGS | VEGAN RECIPE

3   cups fresh fruit, such as sliced strawberries, sliced apricots, sliced peaches, and blueberries (see Tips)

½   cup fresh orange juice

2   tablespoons apricot brandy or other fruit-flavored brandy

Combine the fruit in a medium bowl.

Stir together the orange juice and brandy in a measuring cup. Pour over the fruit.

Cover and refrigerate for at least 2 hours or up to 6 hours before serving.

TIPS | ✿ *Keep fruit at room temperature until it ripens. Once it is ripe, store it in the refrigerator. Wait to wash fruit until just before using.*

Hazelnut Torte
with Chocolate Cream Filling

Marie Wintergerst and I became friends when she attended my culinary presentations on a cruise to French Polynesia. Over dinner, she shared some of her favorite recipes, including this one, which is always her choice to serve for special occasions.

MAKES 8 TO 12 SERVINGS

For the torte

12	eggs, separated		2	tablespoons fine dried bread crumbs
³⁄₄	cup sugar			
2	teaspoons pure vanilla extract			
3	cups very finely ground, peeled hazelnuts (about 10 ounces), see Tips			

For the filling

2	cups heavy cream		¹⁄₂	cup chocolate-flavored liqueur, such as crème de cacao or Godiva, or to taste
¹⁄₃	cup sweetened cocoa powder			
¹⁄₄	cup confectioners' sugar (see Tips)			

To complete the recipe

Fresh strawberries for garnish

Preheat the oven to 350°F. Lightly grease three 9" round cake pans.

To make the torte, use an electric mixer to beat the egg yolks at high speed in a small bowl, adding the sugar gradually until the yolks are lemon-colored. Beat in the vanilla.

Combine the nuts and bread crumbs in a medium bowl.

Beat the egg whites at high speed in a medium bowl until stiff but not dry. Gently fold in the yolks alternately with the hazelnut mixture (see Tips, page 201). Divide the mixture between the prepared pans and lightly spread evenly.

Bake for 20 to 25 minutes, or until a toothpick inserted in the centers comes out clean and the tops are lightly browned. Cool in the pans on racks, then remove from the pans.

To make the filling, use an electric mixer to beat the cream until soft peaks form (see Tips, page 201). Beat in the cocoa powder and confectioners' sugar, then fold in the liqueur.

To complete the recipe, place one cake layer on a plate and spread the top with the filling mixture. Top with the second cake layer and repeat, ending with a topping of the remaining filling. Refrigerate.

Serve wedges of the cake garnished with strawberries.

TIPS | ❧ *Hazelnuts, also called filberts, have a bitter brown skin that is best removed. Heat the nuts at 350°F for 5 to 10 minutes, or until the skins begin to flake. Roll the nuts, one handful at a time, in a clean, thin dishtowel and rub vigorously to remove the papery skin.*

❧ *Confectioners' sugar, also called powdered sugar, is granulated sugar that has been crushed into a fine powder. If necessary, sift before measuring to remove lumps.*

SALAME DOLCE

This decadently rich dessert will amuse your friends, especially those who are vegetarians, be-cause, when sliced, it quite realistically resembles a salami. Serve in thin slices, and, if you like, accompany them with small dollops of sweetened whipped cream and fresh berries. According to my friend and colleague Judy Witts Francini, who shared this recipe, the Italians make this dessert using a small rectangular, flat cookie called Marie. In this country, the cookies are sold as Le Petit Beurre (golden toasted butter biscuits), and they're available in gourmet shops and some super-markets.

MAKES ONE 12" LOG (*about 6 servings*)

	1 stick + 2 tablespoons unsalted butter (5 ounces)	⅓	cup unsweetened or bittersweet cocoa powder
6	ounces Le Petit Beurre cookies (18 cookies)	3	tablespoons Kahlúa, almond-flavored liqueur (such as Amaretto di Saronno), rum, or whiskey
2	egg yolks (see Tips)		
½	cup sugar		

Melt the butter in a small saucepan over low heat. (Or, cut the butter into table-spoon-size pieces and melt in a loosely covered, small glass bowl in the microwave oven on medium power.) Set aside to cool.

In 2 batches, put the cookies in a zip-top bag and crush with a rolling pin. (It's important to use a rolling pin rather than a food processor because the crumbs should remain coarse and inconsistent in size. They will appear to be the fat in the salami.)

Whisk the egg yolks with the sugar in a medium bowl until the sugar is dissolved and the mixture is light-colored and creamy. Stir in the butter, cocoa, and Kahlúa or other liqueur. Add the cookie crumbs and stir until they are evenly incorpo-rated.

Form the mixture into a salami-shaped log, about 12" long and 2" in diameter (or 2 logs, each about 6" long). Wrap the log tightly in plastic wrap and place on a flat sheet in the freezer. After about 20 minutes, remove the log from the freezer and roll it on the countertop to round any flat sides.

Tightly wrapped in plastic wrap, the salami will keep for up to 1 month in the freezer. Before serving, remove the log from the freezer, refrigerate it for 2 hours, and then let it stand at room temperature for about 15 minutes. The log should be firm and still cool for serving.

I like to place the salami on a platter accompanied by a knife, a small bowl of sweetened whipped cream, and berries. Allow your guests to help themselves.

TIPS | ❦ *For this and other uncooked recipes, it's wise to use eggs that have undergone pasteurization to eliminate potential bacteria, including salmonella. You'll find pasteurized eggs along with the refrigerated eggs in most supermarkets.*

If necessary, you can use pasteurized liquid eggs, which come packaged in a carton. One-quarter cup equals 1 egg. (In this recipe, $^1/_4$ cup can be used in place of the 2 egg yolks.)

Limoncello

This recipe comes from my friend Judy Witts Francini, who lives in Florence, where I learned to enjoy the Italian custom of sipping this digestif after dinner. The liqueur is available in many liquor stores, but it's fun to make your own, like the Italians do. As Judy says, "When life gives you lemons . . . make limoncello."

Best stored in the freezer, Limoncello can be served straight up in a tiny chilled glass, or as a palate-cleanser during or after a multicourse meal. It's also delicious mixed with iced tea; and for a special dessert, blend it with ice cream (page 190).

MAKES 3½ CUPS | VEGAN RECIPE

2	cups 100-proof vodka	2	cups water
	Zest of 5 lemons, preferably organic (see Tips)	1½	cups sugar

Combine the vodka and lemon zest in a 1-quart covered glass jar. Let it stand at room temperature for 3 days.

Make a simple syrup by heating the water and sugar in a medium saucepan over medium heat. Stir until the sugar dissolves. Remove from the heat and bring to room temperature.

Stir the syrup into the jar containing the vodka. Pour the mixture through a fine-mesh sieve and discard the lemon zest.

Pour the Limoncello into 1 or more clean glass bottles and cap tightly. Store in the refrigerator or freezer.

TIPS | ❧ *To remove citrus zest, use a zester—a tool with a short, flat blade that has a beveled end and 5 small holes. When drawn firmly over the skin of a citrus fruit, the tool removes thin strips of the colored zest, which contains fragrant oils that add flavor to food. You could also use a microplane: a stainless steel, razor-sharp tool with small, coarse teeth. Or, use a vegetable peeler to remove strips of the zest, and slice into thin strips with a knife. (Whichever method you use, do not strip off the white pith beneath the colored zest; it has a bitter flavor.)*

When using zest in recipes, it's best to choose organic citrus fruits. If you use nonorganic fruit, be sure to scrub it well before zesting to remove any pesticides that may be trapped in the dimples of the skin.

LIMONCELLO ICE CREAM

What could be simpler than to serve this cool, refreshing finale on the deck or patio at sundown?

MAKES 2½ CUPS (*4 servings*)

3   cups good-quality vanilla ice
     cream

½   cup Limoncello (*page 188*) or
     store-bought limoncello

Long, thin strips of lemon zest for
garnish

Blend the ice cream with the limoncello in a blender until smooth. Serve immediately in small liqueur glasses for sipping.

If you prefer, immediately transfer the mixture to a covered container and freeze until firm. Store in the freezer for up to 1 week. Use a small ice cream scoop and serve in dessert bowls.

Garnish the servings with lemon zest strips.

COFFEE-FLAVORED LIQUEUR

You can make your own coffee-flavored liqueur using vodka. The higher the proof, the less flavor the vodka will have, so 100-proof is the best to use. This recipe is easy to multiply. (One winter, I made it by the gallon!) Poured into pretty bottles, it becomes an elegant and tasteful gift that's perfect to share with friends.

MAKES 3 CUPS | VEGAN RECIPE

1 cup sugar	1 teaspoon pure vanilla extract (see Tips)
1 cup water	1 cup 100-proof vodka
¼ cup freeze-dried, granular instant coffee (rather than powdered instant coffee)	

Combine the sugar and water in a small saucepan and bring to a boil, stirring occasionally, over medium heat.

Remove from the heat. Add the coffee and vanilla and stir until the coffee is dissolved. Let cool to room temperature.

Add the vodka and mix well. Pour the mixture into 1 or several clean glass containers. Store in a cool, dark place for 4 weeks, mixing occasionally. (The liqueur can be used within a few days but improves with age.)

TIPS | ❧ *A vanilla bean is the pod of one variety of orchids. The labor-intensive, time-consuming process of curing the pods, which I observed while visiting a plantation on Fiji, justifies their relatively high price. Vanilla extract is produced by macerating chopped beans in an alcohol-water solution in order to extract the flavor; the mixture is then aged for several months. Be sure to purchase the seductively aromatic pure extract rather than imitation vanilla, which is composed entirely of artificial flavors with a harsh quality and a bitter aftertaste.*

Java-Sauced Poached Pears

I love to make this recipe, which I adapted from my friend Fran's creation, in the fall when pears are at their peak of flavor. The elegant sauce, as rich and thick as caramel, has undertones of coffee. This makes the pears and topping delicious on their own, but they're especially tempting served with a small scoop of rich vanilla ice cream.

Makes 6 servings | Vegan recipe (*if served without ice cream*)

For the pears

4	large pears, cored and peeled (see Tips)	1	cup sugar, divided
3	cups water	¼	cup Coffee-Flavored Liqueur (*page 191*) or store-bought Kahlúa
2	tablespoons fresh lemon juice		

For the topping

2	teaspoons packed brown sugar	½	teaspoon instant coffee powder

To prepare the pears, first halve each pear and cut each half into 4 lengthwise slices. Set the slices aside.

Bring the water, lemon juice, and ½ cup of the sugar to a boil in a medium saucepan over medium-high heat. Add the pear slices. When the liquid returns to a boil, reduce the heat to medium-low. Simmer until the pears are easily pierced with the tip of a knife, about 5 minutes. Using a slotted spoon, arrange the pears in a single layer in a baking dish or flat refrigerator container and let them cool to room temperature.

Transfer 1 cup of the pear cooking liquid to a small saucepan. Add the remaining ½ cup of sugar and bring to a boil over medium-high heat. Reduce the heat to medium-low and cook, uncovered, until the sauce becomes light brown, about 20 to 25 minutes. (Watch closely; do not let it become dark brown.)

Remove the saucepan from the heat and stir in the liqueur. Set aside until the sauce is lukewarm, about 10 minutes. Stir the sauce and pour it over the pears. Cover and refrigerate for at least 3 hours or up to 1 day.

To make the topping, combine the brown sugar and coffee powder in a small bowl.

Serve the pears chilled or at room temperature. For each serving, arrange 5 pear slices on a plate and drizzle with about 2 tablespoons of the sauce. Lightly sprinkle the plate with the brown sugar mixture.

TIPS | ❈ *Most pears develop a better flavor and smoother texture when ripened off the tree, so buy them while they are firm. Ripen the pears for 2 to 7 days on your kitchen counter in a loosely closed paper bag or a covered fruit-ripening bowl. To speed ripening, add an apple or banana to the container. Because they ripen from the inside out, most pears do not show ripeness with a color change. Pears used for cooking or baking should be slightly underripe. For eating, the flesh near the stem should yield slightly to gentle pressure. Once ripe, refrigerate unwashed pears in a plastic or paper bag for up to 3 days.*

Baked Peaches
with Almond-Ricotta Topping

Here's the perfect dessert to conclude an Italian meal. In the winter, you can substitute fresh pear halves for the peaches. The fruit, while still warm, is delectable with room-temperature topping. Or, if you prefer, bake the fruit and refrigerate for up to 6 hours. The topping will keep in a covered container in the refrigerator for up to 2 days; it becomes firmer and can be mounded in the hollows of the chilled fruit. Assemble the dessert just before serving.

MAKES 6 SERVINGS

3	peaches, peeled, halved, and pitted (see Tips)	2	tablespoons toasted slivered almonds (see Tips, page 73)
²/₃	cup ricotta cheese (see Tips)	2	tablespoons dried currants (see Tips)
¼	cup semisweet chocolate chips	1	teaspoon grated orange zest
2	tablespoons almond-flavored liqueur, such as Amaretto di Saronno		Sweetened cocoa powder for garnish
2	tablespoons honey		

Preheat the oven to 350°F.

Use a spoon to remove the discolored pulp from the peach halves and discard. Arrange the peaches, cut side up, in a 9" × 9" baking dish. Bake for about 20 minutes, or until they are tender but still hold their shape.

Meanwhile, stir together the remaining ingredients, except the garnish, in a small bowl.

To serve, place the peach halves, cut side up, in small dessert bowls. Serve warm, room temperature, or chilled. Top each peach half with about 2 tablespoons of the ricotta mixture and lightly dust with cocoa powder stirred through a fine-mesh strainer.

TIPS | ❧ *Peak season for peaches is June to August, although they are widely available from May to October. Peaches won't sweeten after being picked, but you can ripen them at room temperature in a paper bag pierced in several places. Add an apple to the bag to speed ripening. Refrigerate ripe peaches in a plastic bag for up to 5 days. For the best flavor, bring them to room temperature before eating. You can peel peaches with a paring knife or vegetable peeler; but for a smoother surface after peeling, blanch peaches in boiling water for 30 seconds, plunge them into ice water, then slip off the skins.*

❧ *Ricotta is made from the whey that remains after the production of such cheeses as provolone and mozzarella. The whey is blended with whole or skim milk. Ricotta, therefore, is not a true cheese because it is not made from curd.*

❧ *Dried currants—actually dried seedless Zante grapes—resemble tiny, dark raisins. You'll find them with dried fruits in the supermarket.*

Broiled Bananas
with Rum-Raisin Sauce

This luscious rum sauce turns the humble banana into a gourmet dessert. After a light meal, add a scoop of creamy, rich vanilla ice cream to complete the euphoria.

MAKES 4 SERVINGS

For the sauce

1	cup fresh orange juice		1	tablespoon cold water
¼	cup dark rum		1	tablespoon cornstarch (see Tips)
2	tablespoons honey			Dash of freshly grated nutmeg (see Tips)
1	tablespoon unsalted butter			
¼	cup golden or dark raisins			

To complete the recipe

4	bananas		Toasted chopped pecans or walnuts (see Tips, page 73) for garnish
1	tablespoon fresh lemon juice		
2	tablespoons unsalted butter, cut into ¼" chunks		

Position the oven broiler rack about 5" from the heating element. Preheat the broiler.

To make the sauce, combine the orange juice, rum, honey, butter, and raisins in a small nonstick saucepan. Stir occasionally over medium heat until the butter melts. Stir together the cold water and cornstarch in a small bowl until smooth, then stir it into the saucepan. Cook, stirring constantly, until the sauce is slightly thickened, about 2 minutes. Stir in the nutmeg, then taste and adjust the seasoning. Remove from the heat and cover to keep warm.

Lightly coat a 9" × 9" baking dish with cooking spray.

To complete the recipe, peel the bananas and cut them in half both lengthwise and crosswise. Arrange the strips, uncut side up, in the baking dish. Drizzle with the lemon juice and dot with the butter.

Broil for about 5 minutes, watching closely, until the bananas are lightly browned.

For each serving, arrange 4 banana sections in a dessert bowl. Drizzle with about ¼ cup of the warm sauce, sprinkle with nuts, and serve immediately.

TIPS | ❦ *Store cornstarch in an airtight container. To use, dissolve in cold liquid, and then stir into a warm liquid near the end of the cooking time. Cook, stirring constantly, until the mixture is thickened, then up to 1 minute more to remove any cornstarch flavor. Do not let the mixture come to a boil.*

❦ *Freshly grated whole nutmeg is more aromatic and flavorful than preground nutmeg. Use a nutmeg grater, which can be purchased in a gourmet shop. Whole nutmeg will keep its flavor for years if stored in a jar in your spice cabinet.*

ORANGES IN HONEY-MARSALA SAUCE

I usually serve this as a refreshing dessert after a filling meal, but it has also received rave reviews as the star of a leisurely brunch. The oranges and syrup can be prepared up to 4 hours before serving. Serve chilled or bring to room temperature.

MAKES 4 SERVINGS | VEGAN RECIPE

¼   cup honey, or ⅓ cup if the oranges are tart (see Tips)

¼   cup water

¼   cup sweet Marsala wine

Zest from 2 oranges

2   tablespoons fresh lemon juice

4   large seedless oranges

Stir together the honey, water, wine, and orange zest in a medium saucepan. Bring to a boil over medium heat. Reduce the heat to medium-low and simmer, uncovered, until the syrup is reduced by about one-third, about 10 minutes. (It will still be thin in consistency.) Remove from the heat and set aside to cool. Stir in the lemon juice.

Slice off about ½" from the top (stem end) and bottom of each orange. To remove the remaining zest and white pith, stand each orange on end and cut downward all around, cutting beneath the white pith, to remove the rind in strips.

Arrange the oranges in a flat dish and pour the cooled syrup over the oranges. Cover with plastic wrap and refrigerate.

Place each orange in a dessert bowl and drizzle with the syrup, then top each orange with some of the orange zest in the sauce. Serve with a serrated knife and fork. (Or, if you prefer, cut the oranges crosswise into ¼"-thick slices, arrange on plates, and drizzle with the syrup.)

TIPS | ✽ *Generally, the darker the color, the stronger the flavor of honey. Store honey in an airtight container at room temperature. If it crystallizes, place the jar in hot water until the crystals dissolve. Or, microwave the honey container (metal lid removed) on medium power for 5 to 10 seconds.*

FRESH PEACH MOUSSE

Using these proportions, feel free to substitute another fruit, such as strawberries, mango, or papaya, or your favorite combination. The result is fluffy, light, and oh, so satisfying.

MAKES 6 SERVINGS

1½ cups puréed fresh peaches (about 4 peeled and pitted peaches)

½ cup sugar

¼ cup orange-flavored liqueur, such as Cointreau

¼ cup water

1 envelope unflavored gelatin (see Tips)

1 cup heavy cream

½ teaspoon pure almond extract

Small sprigs of fresh mint for garnish

Blend the peaches, sugar, and liqueur in a blender or food processor until smooth.

Pour the water into a small saucepan and sprinkle the gelatin over it. Let it stand until the gelatin softens, about 3 minutes.

Meanwhile, use electric beaters to beat the cream in a medium bowl until soft peaks form (see Tips). Gently fold in the almond extract.

Cook the gelatin mixture over low heat, stirring constantly until the gelatin dissolves, about 3 minutes. Let cool slightly and then stir it into the peach mixture. Gently fold (see Tips) this mixture into the whipped cream.

Spoon the mousse into individual serving dishes or into a medium-size, flat-bottomed bowl. Cover and chill until set, about 2 hours. Serve within 36 hours of chilling.

Garnish the servings with mint sprigs.

TIPS | ❧ *Wrapped airtight and kept in a cool, dry place, gelatin will last indefinitely. It is important to soften the gelatin in cold liquid, which dissolves the gelatin granules. The mixture should then be warmed over low heat; do not let it boil. Gelatin sets rapidly as it cools, so add to the base mixture while it is still warm.*

❧ *Store cream in the coldest part of the refrigerator, where it will last for about 1 week past the sell-by date. For the best results, when whipping cream, start with everything cold: the cream, the bowls, and the beaters.*

Generally, when a recipe calls for whipped cream, it should be in soft peaks that mound easily on a spoon and fall off with 1 shake. Firm peaks appear slightly granular around the edges. Just a step away is overbeaten cream, which is the consistency of butter. To restore overbeaten whipped cream, add a little more cold, liquid heavy cream and fold it in using a rubber spatula.

❧ *Folding is the key to maintaining volume when adding yolks or other ingredients to beaten cream or stiff egg whites. Gently whisk or stir a small portion, about one-fourth, of the whipped egg ingredient into the base ingredients to lighten the mixture. Mound the remaining beaten ingredient over the base. (Putting the heavy base on top will press out the air.) Using a wide rubber spatula, combine the mixtures with a downward stroke into the center of the bowl, circling across the bottom, up the side, and over the top of the mixture. Come up through the center every few strokes, rotating the bowl frequently as you fold. Fold just until the ingredients are combined. Overworking will deflate the whipped cream or egg whites.*

Rum-Marinated Fruit Brochettes

A Bermudian shared this recipe with me on a recent visit to the beautiful island. The well-known, local rum is my first choice, but any dark rum will do. While the original version called for guava paste, which for most of us is difficult to find, you can substitute jelly made from tropical fruits, available in most supermarkets.

MAKES 20 BROCHETTES | VEGAN RECIPE

For the marinade

½	cup fresh orange juice	1	teaspoon minced fresh ginger
¼	cup guava paste or jelly made from tropical fruits	½	teaspoon curry powder
		2	tablespoons fresh lime juice
2	tablespoons Dijon mustard (see Tips)	1	tablespoon dark rum

For the fruit

40 chunks (1") of assorted tropical fruits, such as mango, papaya, pineapple, loquat, kiwifruit, and star fruit

Soak ten 6" bamboo skewers in cold water for about 30 minutes.

To make the marinade, blend the orange juice, guava paste, mustard, ginger, and curry powder in a blender until smooth. Transfer the mixture to a small saucepan, cover, and simmer over low heat for about 10 minutes. Remove from the heat and let cool. Stir in the lime juice and rum.

To assemble the fruit, thread 4 pieces on each of the skewers. Arrange in a single row in a shallow, flat-bottomed refrigerator container. Pour the marinade over the fruit. Cover and refrigerate, turning the skewers occasionally, for at least 3 hours or overnight.

Just before serving, adjust the oven broiler rack to 4" or 5" from the heating element. Preheat the broiler. Arrange the skewers in a single layer on a foil-lined jelly roll pan. Broil for 2 minutes, or until thoroughly heated and lightly browned in some places.

Serve the brochettes warm or at room temperature.

TIPS | ✖ *Dijon mustard, which originated in Dijon, France, is made from brown mustard seeds, spices, grape juice, and white wine. It's spicier and more flavorful than ordinary yellow mustard.*

BERRIES ROYALE

Come berry season, this simple, light, and stylish dessert adds instant elegance to your meal. It's not necessary to use true Champagne. A more affordable sparkling wine, such as Spanish Cava, will do just fine.

MAKES 4 SERVINGS | VEGAN RECIPE

2   cups fresh berries, such as blueberries, strawberries, raspberries, blackberries, or a combination

½   cup chilled dry Champagne, sparkling dry white wine such as Cava, or semisweet sparkling white wine such as Prosecco

2   tablespoons crème de cassis

Arrange the berries in parfait glasses, wine glasses, champagne flutes, or martini glasses. Pour the champagne over the berries and top with the crème de cassis. Serve immediately.

Strawberries and Grapes in Kirsch

This is a simple, sweet, refreshing dessert—perfect after a big meal. Kirsch, a cherry-flavored liqueur, adds fruitiness and just the right amount of residual alcohol.

Makes 4 servings | Vegan recipe

¼ cup Kirsch

¼ cup fresh lemon juice

¼ cup sugar

1½ cups sliced fresh strawberries

1½ cups seedless red grapes, halved lengthwise (see Tips)

Fresh mint sprigs for garnish

Combine the Kirsch, lemon juice, and sugar in a small saucepan. Stir over low heat, just until the sugar dissolves. Remove from the heat and let stand until room temperature.

Combine the strawberries and grapes in a medium bowl. Stir in the Kirsch mixture. Refrigerate in a covered container for at least 2 or up to 8 hours.

To serve, spoon the cold mixture into clear, stemmed glasses and garnish with mint sprigs.

TIPS | ❧ *When shopping for grapes, look for full clusters attached to green and pliable stems. Refrigerate them in a loosely closed plastic bag for up to 1 week. Wash in cool water just before using and blot dry with paper towels.*

GINGERED FRUIT

Crystallized ginger is the ace in the hole that adds an enticing zip to the orange-scented fruits of summer.

MAKES 4 SERVINGS | VEGAN RECIPE

¼ cup fresh orange juice

3 tablespoons orange-flavored liqueur, such as Cointreau

1 teaspoon sugar

2 tablespoons minced crystallized ginger (see Tips)

3 cups fresh berries, such as blueberries, raspberries, and sliced strawberries

Sprigs of fresh mint for garnish

Combine the orange juice, liqueur, and sugar in a medium bowl. Stir until the sugar dissolves. Stir in the ginger. Add the fruit and toss.

Refrigerate the mixture in a covered container for at least 2 or up to 8 hours before serving. Serve cold in clear glass dessert cups and garnish with mint sprigs.

TIPS | ❧ *Crystallized, or candied, ginger has been cooked in a sugar syrup and coated with coarse sugar. This sweet ginger is generally used as a confection or added to desserts. Store it in your spice cabinet in a jar with a tight-fitting lid.*

PEAR APPLESAUCE
WITH ALMOND LIQUEUR

This is applesauce for adults. Almond liqueur adds a little kick to this light dessert, do-ahead snack, or portion of a brunch menu. It can be refrigerated for up to 3 days.

MAKES 2 CUPS (*4 servings*) | VEGAN RECIPE

2	Granny Smith apples, peeled, cored, and cut into ½" chunks	1	tablespoon packed brown sugar (see Tips)
2	Bartlett pears, peeled, cored, and cut into ½" chunks	2	tablespoons almond-flavored liqueur, such as Amaretto di Saronno
¼	cup water		

Combine the apples, pears, and water in a medium saucepan. Cover and cook over low heat until very tender, about 15 minutes.

Use a spoon to mash the fruit to the desired consistency, chunky or smooth. Add the sugar and almond liqueur and stir until the sugar is dissolved.

Serve at room temperature or refrigerate in a covered container and serve later, chilled.

TIPS | ❧ *Brown sugar is made of white sugar combined with molasses, which gives it a soft texture. It is available in both light and dark varieties; the lighter the color, the milder the flavor. Store brown sugar in a tightly closed container at room temperature. Hardened brown sugar can be softened by placing an apple wedge in the jar or bag of sugar. Seal it tightly for 1 or 2 days, then remove the fruit.*

Strawberry-Shiraz Sorbet

So simple. So captivating. Serve this ruby-colored sorbet in stemmed glasses as a light dessert, or offer it between courses of a dinner menu to refresh the palate.

MAKES 8 SERVINGS | VEGAN RECIPE

2 cups sliced strawberries (see Tips)	1 cup Shiraz or other full-bodied, ripe-jammy red wine
½ cup sugar	
2 tablespoons fresh lemon juice	

Purée the strawberries, sugar, and lemon juice in a blender until smooth. Stir in the wine.

Pour the mixture into an ungreased 9" × 9" baking dish. Cover and freeze for at least 8 hours, or until firm.

Before serving, let stand at room temperature for about 5 minutes.

Use a small ice cream scoop to assemble the servings.

TIPS | ❄ *Choose brightly colored strawberries with their hulls attached. Just before using, be sure to rinse strawberries,* **then** *hull them. Hulled strawberries will absorb water like a sponge.*

WATERMELON POPTAILS

Among the splendid gifts of summer is the watermelon. In addition to savoring the juicy wedges straight from the market, try making these colorful, refreshing popsicles for adults using the plastic molds seasonally stocked in gourmet shops and in the kitchen department of your local discount store. Buy several sets, so you can multiply the recipe. For quick preparation, look for seedless watermelon, available during the summer in most supermarkets.

MAKES 4 SERVINGS | VEGAN RECIPE

2	cups seedless red watermelon in ½" cubes (see Tips)
2	tablespoons sugar
2	tablespoons fresh lime juice

2	tablespoons lemon vodka
1	tablespoon orange-flavored liqueur, such as Cointreau

Purée all of the ingredients in a blender until smooth. (If necessary, first remove the scattered watermelon seeds.)

Fill 4 popsicle forms with the mixture and freeze until firm. Or, you can use 2- or 3-ounce paper cups: Fill them with the watermelon mixture and freeze for 1 to 2 hours until slushy. Then insert wooden craft sticks or plastic spoons to serve as handles and freeze the mixture solid.

TIPS | ❧ *Watermelons are available from May to September but are at their peak from mid-June to late August. Store a whole watermelon in the refrigerator for up to 1 week. Cut pieces should be wrapped in plastic and refrigerated for no more than a day or two.*

Citrus-Mint Granitas

This refreshing, icy treat will melt on your tongue like snow. Serve it as a palate-pleasing intermezzo between dinner courses or as a light dessert. Be sure to scrub the oranges well before zesting. And it's a nice touch to chill the serving glasses in advance.

MAKES 8 SERVINGS | VEGAN RECIPE

1	cup Gewürztraminer or other medium-bodied, sweet and fruity white wine
1	cup water
⅓	cup sugar

	Grated zest of 2 oranges
1	cup fresh orange juice
½	cup fresh lemon juice
2	large sprigs of fresh mint + 8 small sprigs (see Tips) for garnish

Combine the wine, water, and sugar in a medium saucepan. Stir occasionally over medium heat until the sugar melts. Remove from the heat. Stir in the orange zest and the orange and lemon juices.

Pour the mixture into a 9" × 9" baking dish and immerse the 2 large mint sprigs in the mixture. Cover with plastic wrap and let stand at room temperature for 2 hours. Remove the mint sprigs.

Cover the dish and place in the freezer for an hour or two until the mixture has frozen around the edges. Remove the container from the freezer and scrape the mixture with a fork, moving it from the edge into the center. Repeat this 3 or 4 times, about once per hour, until the mixture is completely frozen and the ice crystals are fluffy.

Transfer the mixture to a covered freezer container and freeze for an hour longer to dry the crystals. It's best to serve the granita within a few days, but the mixture will keep for up to 1 month.

To serve, scrape again with a fork and spoon the granita into stemmed glasses. Garnish with the remaining small mint sprigs. Granita melts quickly, so serve it immediately.

Variation: If you don't have time to scrape the mixture with a fork, let it freeze completely in the pan. Just before serving, remove the pan from the freezer and let stand at room temperature for a few minutes. Break the mixture into chunks and purée in a blender. The result will be less flaky and smoother, like a sorbet.

TIPS | ❧ *There are over 30 species of mint; the most popular are spearmint, the kind most frequently found in supermarkets, and peppermint, the more pungent of the two. Choose leaves that are evenly colored with no sign of wilting. Store the bunch, stems down, in a glass of water with a plastic bag over the leaves. Refrigerate for up to 1 week, changing the water every 2 days.*

HOT FUDGE SAUCE

This sensuous sauce turns plain-Jane ice cream into gourmet hot fudge sundaes—or banana splits—for adults. It can lend its elegance to cakes, poached pears, or crepes.

The sauce will keep for up to 1 week in a covered container in the refrigerator. It thickens as it chills; before serving, reheat to its creamy consistency in a double boiler or in the microwave oven on low power.

MAKES ¾ CUP

4	ounces semisweet chocolate, coarsely chopped	2	tablespoons B & B or other flavored liqueur, such as almond-flavored liqueur (Amaretto di Saronno) or hazelnut-flavored liqueur (Frangelico)
½	cup heavy cream or half-and-half		

Combine the chocolate, cream, and B & B or other liqueur in the top pan of a double boiler over simmering water (see Tips). Stir constantly as the chocolate melts and until the sauce is smooth, about 5 minutes. Serve warm.

TIPS | ❧ *A double boiler is a double pan, the smaller one sitting partway inside the larger. The lower pot is used to hold simmering water, which gently heats the mixture in the top pot. Adjust the level of the water so that it does not touch the bottom of the top pan. Use a double boiler to cook heat-sensitive foods, such as custards, delicate sauces, and chocolate. If you don't have a double boiler, use a stainless-steel bowl set over a saucepan of simmering water.*

Raspberry-Merlot Sauce

Red wine and raspberries is a marriage made in heaven. This ruby sauce will keep in a covered container in the refrigerator for up to 2 weeks. Thin with water, if necessary, and serve over poached pears, fresh pineapple rings, ice cream, or innumerable other desserts. I especially like to pair it with Hot Fudge Sauce (opposite page) to create a spectacular ice cream sundae. And one of my favorite summer desserts is vanilla ice cream, topped with fresh peach slices and drizzled with this lovely sauce. Voilà! A luscious peach Melba. You'll find this sauce as an important component in the Honeydew Melon Salad (page 104), where it adds both flavor and color to the impressive presentation.

MAKES ¾ CUP | VEGAN RECIPE

4 cups (two 12-ounce packages) frozen unsweetened raspberries, thawed	1½ cups Merlot or other full-bodied, plummy red wine
	1 cup sugar

Combine all the ingredients in a small saucepan. Bring to a boil over high heat. Reduce the heat to medium and simmer, uncovered, over medium-low heat until the mixture is thick and reduced to about 1 cup, about 30 minutes. As the sauce cooks, stir occasionally to prevent scorching.

Strain the sauce through a coarse sieve atop a mixing bowl. As it drains, stir the sauce occasionally with a wooden spoon. Discard the seeds.

INDEX

Underscored page references indicate tips or boxed text.

skinning, <u>185</u>
toasting, <u>73</u>
Herbs. *See also* Basil
    bouquet garni, about, <u>163</u>
    chives, about, <u>79</u>
    Citrus-Mint Granitas, 210–11
    dill, about, <u>159</u>
    dried, in recipes, <u>169</u>
    dried, storing, <u>169</u>
    fresh, adding to recipes, <u>169</u>
    fresh, cutting, <u>145</u>
    fresh, storing, <u>135</u>
    Fresh Herb Cream Sauce, 33
    Fried Sage, 115
    mint, about, <u>211</u>
    parsley, about, <u>147</u>
    robust and tender, <u>129</u>
    rosemary, about, <u>61</u>
    sage, about, <u>143</u>
Honey, about, <u>199</u>

Ice cream
    Limoncello Ice Cream, 190
Ingredients, 17–19

Jelly
    Red Wine Jelly, 42
Julienne, <u>157</u>

Kale, <u>137</u>
    Tequila-Braised Kale, 136–37

Leeks, <u>61</u>
    Pasta Primavera, 156–57
    Yukon Gold Potato–Leek Soup, 68–69
Lemons, <u>189</u>
    Citrus-Mint Granitas, 210–11
    Limoncello, 188
    Limoncello Ice Cream, 190
Lentils, <u>131</u>
    Acorn Squash and Red Lentils with Toasted
        Walnuts, 130–31
    Curried Lentil Soup, 55
    Zucchini Stuffed with Lentils and Tomatoes,
        158–59
Liqueurs. *See also* Brandies; Liqueurs, flavored
    cooking with, 14

Liqueurs, flavored
    Baked Peaches with Almond-Ricotta Topping,
        194–95
    buying, 14–15
    Coffee-Flavored Liqueur, 191
    Cranberry Margarita Relish, 43
    Fresh Herb Cream Sauce, 33
    Fresh Peach Mousse, 200–201
    Gingered Fruit, 206
    Hazelnut Torte with Chocolate Cream Filling,
        184–85
    Hot Fudge Sauce, 212
    Java-Sauced Poached Pears, 192–93
    Limoncello, 188
    Pear and Almond Tart, 178–79
    Pear Applesauce with Almond Liqueur, 207
    Pears Poached in Crème de Cassis, 87
    Salame Dolce, 186–87
    Strawberries and Grapes in Kirsch, 205
    Triple Chocolate–Cassis Brownies, 180–81
    types of, 14–15
    Watermelon Poptails, 209
Liquors, 16. *See also* Rum; Tequila; Vodka
    cooking with, 14

Macerating, 7–8
Main courses
    Acorn Squash and Red Lentils with Toasted
        Walnuts, 130–31
    Asparagus-Cashew Stir-Fry, 132–33
    Bow Ties with Marsala-Mushroom Sauce,
        150–51
    Cannellini Bean Bourguignonne, 128–29
    Carrot Patties with Orange-Sherry Sauce, 160–61
    Fettuccine with Cremini Mushrooms, 146–47
    Gingered Squash Risotto with Glazed Pecans and
        Fried Sage, 113–14
    Lasagna Rolls with Roasted Bell Pepper Sauce,
        144–45
    Linguine with Morels and Asparagus, 140–41
    Pasta Primavera, 156–57
    Penne with Rainbow Peppers and Red Onion,
        152–53
    Penne with Triple-Tomato Pesto, 148–49
    Penne with Yams and Mushrooms, 142–43
    Polenta Pizza, 122
    Polenta Triangles, 120–21

Conversion Chart

These equivalents have been slightly rounded to make measuring easier.

VOLUME MEASUREMENTS

U.S.	Imperial	Metric
¼ tsp	–	1 ml
½ tsp	–	2 ml
1 tsp	–	5 ml
1 Tbsp	–	15 ml
2 Tbsp (1 oz)	1 fl oz	30 ml
¼ cup (2 oz)	2 fl oz	60 ml
⅓ cup (3 oz)	3 fl oz	80 ml
½ cup (4 oz)	4 fl oz	120 ml
⅔ cup (5 oz)	5 fl oz	160 ml
¾ cup (6 oz)	6 fl oz	180 ml
1 cup (8 oz)	8 fl oz	240 ml

WEIGHT MEASUREMENTS

U.S.	Metric
1 oz	30 g
2 oz	60 g
4 oz (¼ lb)	115 g
5 oz (⅓ lb)	145 g
6 oz	170 g
7 oz	200 g
8 oz (½ lb)	230 g
10 oz	285 g
12 oz (¾ lb)	340 g
14 oz	400 g
16 oz (1 lb)	455 g
2.2 lb	1 kg

LENGTH MEASUREMENTS

U.S.	Metric
¼"	0.6 cm
½"	1.25 cm
1"	2.5 cm
2"	5 cm
4"	11 cm
6"	15 cm
8"	20 cm
10"	25 cm
12" (1')	30 cm

PAN SIZES

U.S.	Metric
8" cake pan	20 × 4 cm sandwich or cake tin
9" cake pan	23 × 3.5 cm sandwich or cake tin
11" × 7" baking pan	28 × 18 cm baking tin
13" × 9" baking pan	32.5 × 23 cm baking tin
15" × 10" baking pan	38 × 25.5 cm baking tin (Swiss roll tin)
1½ qt baking dish	1.5 liter baking dish
2 qt baking dish	2 liter baking dish
2 qt rectangular baking dish	30 × 19 cm baking dish
9" pie plate	22 × 4 or 23 × 4 cm pie plate
7" or 8" springform pan	18 or 20 cm springform or loose-bottom cake tin
9" × 5" loaf pan	23 × 13 cm or 2 lb narrow loaf tin or pâté tin

TEMPERATURES

Fahrenheit	Centigrade	Gas
140°	60°	–
160°	70°	–
180°	80°	–
225°	105°	¼
250°	120°	½
275°	135°	1
300°	150°	2
325°	160°	3
350°	180°	4
375°	190°	5
400°	200°	6
425°	220°	7
450°	230°	8
475°	245°	9
500°	260°	–